THE
BACKWARD
LIFE

In Pursuit of an
Uncommon Faith

JARROD JONES

Revell
Grand Rapids, Michigan

© 2006 by Jarrod Jones

Published by Fleming H. Revell
a division of Baker Publishing Group
P.O. Box 6287, Grand Rapids, MI 49516-6287
www.revellbooks.com

Printed in the United States of America

Library of Congress Cataloging-in-Publication Data
Jones, Jarrod, 1972–
    The backward life : in pursuit of an uncommon faith / Jarrod Jones.
      p. cm.
    Includes bibliographical references.
    ISBN 10: 0-8007-3144-1 (pbk.)
    ISBN 978-0-8007-3144-1 (pbk.)
    1. Christian life. I. Title
    BV4501.3.J653 2006
    248.4—dc22   2006007946

To my wife, Christie.
Your love for me is so unselfish that it's backward.
I love you so much it hurts.

back-ward\ 'bak-wərd\ *adv* 2a: in a reverse
or contrary direction or way

Contents

A Foreword on Backward

Jarrod Jones was my hero when we were little kids growing up in the small town of Clanton, Alabama. I looked up to him, both figuratively and literally. He was only a year older than me, but he always seemed to be two feet taller than me.

When I first moved up from tee ball to Little League, I was scared to death. Here I was, surrounded by a bunch of guys older, bigger, and better than me, and I was supposed to hit a fastball? The coach asked me to try out first base, which I'd never played before, and I was thinking, *Great . . . here's another new thing I've got to worry about!*

Sounds kind of silly now, but when you're a little kid, this stuff is traumatic. Luckily for me, the starter at first base was a kind and encouraging guy. You guessed it: Jarrod.

He calmed me down and started teaching me the ropes of first base, letting me know there was nothing to worry about, showing me what to do when the ball was hit—positioning my feet, taking cut-off throws from the outfield, and of course the most important thing, not dropping the ball. Jarrod was an all-star baseball player, and I only played first base when he was pitching. But that didn't bother me in the least. I would learn from him what I could, and

9

the next year he would move up to another league, and I would have the opportunity to start at first base.

We did this for a few years and never had any unhealthy competition between us. Though Jarrod was much better than me, he never once made me feel inferior to him. I was so glad to be his friend, teammate, and biggest cheerleader (well, maybe second to his parents).

I moved from Alabama to metro Atlanta after my freshman year of high school and lost contact with Jarrod for a few years. Like him, I grew up in the church and was a good little Christian boy, but as my high school years approached, I started doing my own thing. Don't get me wrong; I was still a believer. I just wasn't completely living my life for Jesus.

To make a long story short, I rededicated my life to the Lord at the end of my senior year in high school. I started realizing that when I tried to live my life for myself, I wasn't having much of a life at all. Jesus said not only that he is "the way, the truth, and the life" but also "I've come to this world to give you life and to give it to you abundantly!" So when we are living without him, we are not really "living" at all. We're only dying.

There lies the great paradox of Christianity.

It's not until we die to ourselves and start living for Jesus that we receive real, amazing, abundant life. This is exactly what my brother Jarrod is trying to explain in this book. *The Backward Life* shares many encouraging, uplifting, challenging, and funny stories as examples of how we can all have that abundant life when we learn to die to ourselves, love God with all our heart, and love others as we love ourselves.

I'm happy to say that after years of not keeping in touch, Jarrod and I reconnected. He shared with me his testimony of how God had taken what the world would see as a great life but in all actuality was an empty one and made it into an abundant life that is passionate for God.

How great it is to find an old friend. For some of you, reading this book will be that reconnection with the old friend whom you haven't spent much quality time with in a while. For others it will be an introduction to someone who will literally change your life for the better.

Jesus has changed my life, he has changed my good friend Jarrod's life, and if you give him the chance, Jesus will change yours too. I am truly honored to have been asked to write a foreword for Jarrod's book. I look forward to hearing of the many lives that will be encouraged and changed by his words. Jarrod Jones was my hero when we were little kids. He still is.

Mac Powell
lead vocalist, Third Day

Acknowledgments

I offer my most heartfelt appreciation to the Vertical Ministries family for their unwavering loyalty to me, love for me, and belief in me. You are adored friends. You have proven over and over again your hearts for ministry—not business but love for people; not bookings but passion for Jesus. Thank you for your sacrifice. It is an honor serving with you.

To my wife, Christie—thank you for reading over my work time and time again, offering counsel, suggestions, and direction. You are so wise.

To Mom, Dad, Tyree, Kevin, Mattie, and Josie (my immediate family)—I understand that you'll never write a book or speak from a platform, but your experiences, sacrifice, wisdom, devotion, and love thread everything I do. I love you.

To my treasured friend Bobbi Brandenberg—your servant's heart is unmatched. Your love for Christie and me is treasured. As I have said a thousand times, "Thank you for everything."

To our young marrieds group at Shades Mountain Independent Church, who embraced Christie and me with all their hearts when we first showed up at the church doorstep—you all continue to nurture us and teach us in so many ways. Thank you for your support, love, wisdom, and prayers. Thank you for taking care of Christie while I'm on the road. You are all a gift from God. We love you.

To Bob Moon, who was my youth pastor when I was a teenager, a father figure when I was a young adult, a close friend today, and a mentor always—our countless hours of discussion about life, ministry, Scripture, people, and struggles echo throughout this book.

To Joel Engle—from the first day I shared the vision for this book with you, you have pushed me and pushed me to get it done and into the culture. Thank you for your investment in me. As you say to me, you are a good brother.

To David and Jennifer Nasser, who gave great insight and advice on different aspects of this book—thank you both for caring about this work.

To Mac Powell—thank you for your love and support.

To all my fellow ministers, pastors, youth pastors, teachers, and servants of Jesus—thank you for persevering in the front lines of ministry to which God has called you. Your partnerships in ministry are savored. I can't wait to serve you again in the years to come.

Lord Jesus, you are beautifully backward, gloriously wounding, and passionately loving. You loved me when I didn't love you. You loved me even when it hurt. I want to be just like you, Jesus. Thank you for first loving me, so that I might love you. And I do . . . so very much.

1

What Am I Made For?

Must have the precious.

Gollum in
The Lord of the Rings

I looked like a Q-tip in junior high school—so pale my skin seemed to have a bluish tint, and with a big wad of white, curly hair on top. I went mostly unnoticed, was picked last for some sports, and was scared to death of females. But something happened between my eighth- and ninth-grade years. I didn't see anyone all summer, and when I returned to school I was a head taller than everyone. I remember guys saying, "Dude, what'd you eat all summer?"

Thanks to my height, I was convinced to go out for the high school basketball team. Expectations ran high. My first game, in front of two high schools, I got my first rebound and went up strong to score my first two points. I ran down the court awaiting the roar of the fans, but there was only silence—then laughter. I realized with horror that I had shot into the wrong goal. I was devastated and henceforth labeled a "dork" for an entire year.

But things began to change as I progressed through high school. I grew a few more inches, gained some coordination, and added some basketball skills. By my junior and senior years, I was popular, a star athlete. I drove a sports car, was voted Mr. CCHS (Chilton County High School) by the high school student body, and dated Ms. CCHS. I was the life of the party and had a posse of guy and girl friends called The Coolin' Crew and Their Little Sisters (okay, you can stop laughing now). I got basketball scholarships—first to a junior college, then to a Division I university—continuing on in popularity, academics, and athletic success. And the girls! Oh my, the girls. I'm ashamed to confess that I took advantage of many offers that came my way, and some obliged my offers as well, if you know what I mean.

It was all about "me." "Me" was my "precious." "Me" was my god. I became what every teenager, college student, and twentysomething wanted to be. I reveled in the attention and the lifestyle. I had only one problem: I was sick of "me."

I grew up in a Christian family. I had to go to church every Sunday, no excuses. I hated church; I thought it was boring and cheesy. I was the little kid who knew all the verses and all the church answers. I viewed God as an angry and bitter tyrant, yet the thought of Jesus was beautiful to me. I appreciated his sacrifice on the cross. I think I truly loved Jesus but just didn't want to obey him. In high school, my Christian life, or lack thereof, could be summed up by a button that I pinned to the visor of my car: "How much sin can I get away with and still go to heaven?" I wanted to live a life centered on "me." Popularity, basketball, and girls were the trinity I lived for. No matter how much attention I got or how many balls I dunked, three-pointers I scored, beers I drank, or girls I "dated," I was haunted by misery, emptiness, and an unsatisfied life.

I clearly remember an experience at a Baylor University basketball tournament where God began to break my heart. During the pre-tournament banquet, I was named an all-star student athlete by Jim Nantz of CBS Sports. Later we met in the lobby of our hotel, and he invited me up to his hotel room to hang out for a few minutes while he took care of some pressing business. We chatted about basketball and my future. Before I left I asked for his autograph to prove I'd spent time with him. He penned his name on a CBS Sports cap and handed me a business card for a clothing line he was putting out with his old college roommate, pro golfer Fred Couples.

I giddily walked out of his room and into the elevator. Once the doors closed, I read the words he had signed: "Jarrod, thanks for being a good role model. Jim Nantz."

Just one problem: I was anything *but* a good role model. Everyone within an arm's reach of my life thought I was the perfect young, popular, successful, Christian student-athlete. But anyone close to me, especially me, knew I was all about my "self." I was plastic. Though there was nothing spiritual about Jim Nantz's words, God used them to begin drawing me to himself.

After college, still searching for that elusive happiness and satisfaction, I developed a new blueprint for happiness. My goals were to get a nice job, purchase a new sports car, get married, adopt a Chihuahua, and buy a new Harley, a new boat, and a big house with a big deck and a big garage to house my new Harley. Even in pursuing and getting some of these things, I was still left with an abyss in my gut. Why? Because I wasn't made for those things.

I'll share more about my past later, but let's hit the pause button here. What does your blueprint for happiness look like? Though I didn't really put this together at the time, my focus on buying, achieving, and succeeding acted as painkillers for what I most hurt for in my life: peace, relief, fulfillment, joy, purpose, unconditional love—the stuff of life that careers and Harleys can't give.

Have you been chasing after the "stuff" of the world in search of that satisfaction that comes from achieving what you were made for? It's easy to stay caught up in the thrill of the chase. But the chase will never end. It's rewarding to achieve and accumulate. But the shine will always fade before you, the attention turn from you, and the applause dissolve around you. What do you believe you are made for? What are you pursuing to distract you and numb you from your need for God? Surf the web of your thoughts, your passions, your relationships, your time, and yes, your money—and you will reach the homepage of that which you have believed you are made for.

There's a story in the Bible in which a teacher of the law happened upon a group of religious leaders who were bent on trapping Jesus. These leaders made every attempt to expose Jesus with their cunning questions each time a crowd gathered. If they could get Jesus to criticize the government or break religious laws, then they could have him arrested. Jealousy ruled among these leaders. Jesus was stealing their show. He was becoming a threat to the status quo. He was a menace to their enjoyment of power, authority, and an esteemed lifestyle.

One would think that, upon hearing this *O'Reilly Factor*–like debate, the teacher of the law might have been taken aback by Jesus' answers. After all, he heard them debating and recognized that "[Jesus] had answered them well."

The questions with which they were bombarding Jesus had to do with taxes, marriage, remarriage, and heaven. I can't really speak for the teacher of the law, but I wonder if he was tired of this philosophical stuff and wanted to get to the meat of life and existence. I wonder if he finally recognized that his power, and authority, and esteemed lifestyle had left him empty. So, upon a pause in the debate, the teacher of the law clears his throat and asks, "Of all the commandments, which is the most important one?" (Mark 12:28).

Could his question be one of searching? Translated in today's language, could he be asking, "What is it that should consume my life? What is the purpose of my existence? What is it that I should bank my life on every morning when I wake up and every night when I lie down? What am I made for?"

I bet a hush came over the crowd when they heard this question. You could probably hear the "shhhhhhs" all over the place. This may not be a *Jeopardy* question, but it is a sincere, searching appeal for truth. Consider that perhaps this isn't a sneering question to back

Jesus into a corner but a seeking man's plea to get his life out of the corner. Does that hit home for you?

Do you think Jesus smiled when he heard the question? This man had just "clicked online" to Jesus' heart. Though he asked Jesus about the greatest commandment, little did he know that within the greatest commandment Jesus would reveal the greatest fulfillment.

"This is the most important," Jesus answered (everyone's leaning in now . . .).

> Hear, O Israel! The Lord our God is one Lord. And you shall love the Lord your God with all your heart, with all your soul, with all your mind, and with all your strength.
>
> Mark 12:29–30 HCSB

I imagine everyone just squinted their eyes and stared at Jesus. "This is nothing new. We've been taught this since Vacation Bible School at the temple!" they say. And that's precisely our problem too: we've heard it all our lives, but we haven't believed it. And that's precisely the reason we haven't obeyed it. We may say one thing but do another. We act and behave according to what we really believe.

But Jesus wasn't finished. "The second is"—there go the "shhh-hhhs" again—"You shall love your neighbor as yourself. There is no other commandment greater than these" (Mark 12:31 HCSB).

Just two sentences . . . that's it. That's all. In two sentences, Jesus gave the key to life. Barnes & Noble, Books-A-Million, Borders, and even Christian bookstores in America are lined with aisles of books by authors attempting to answer the "What am I made for?" question with self-help, self-esteem, self-love, and self-health. Think about this: maybe the reason so many self-help books continue to be published and purchased is because they aren't working. They never truly satisfy that mysterious, voracious craving within us for something better, something more, and something perfect.

Notice that in this great commandment Jesus doesn't mention one word about "self." As a matter of fact, he pointed in opposite directions from "self." I'm convinced that if Jesus lived in America today, you'd never discover a self-help book authored by him, nor a self-help talk show hosted by him—Christian or non-Christian. Jesus is the antithesis of our "self" worship. We've got a good handle on the self-matters, self-help, and self-love. What we don't have a handle on is what we're truly designed for: Jesus' commands to love your God and love your neighbor as yourself. Jesus' answer is not the love of self but the love for God and love for others. This is the key to freedom, the key to joy, the key to fulfillment, the key to purpose. The key to life is that we're not made for "self," we're made for God—and made to give away our lives to other people.

Backward, huh?

After having listened to the tapes, read the books, watched the talk shows, and exhausted yourself trying to improve "you," aren't you just tired? Tired in your soul?

Are you ready to quit living for yourself? Well, of course you're not. Neither am I. As Bill O'Reilly puts it, "the spin stops here." Granted, we need to love ourselves as God loves us. But let's get honest—we love ourselves way too much. And that is precisely the problem.

2

Me, Me, Me

"All Eyez on Me."

song title, 2Pak
(Tupac Shakur)

Afew years ago, I boarded a plane and found myself seated next
to a teenage girl whose face looked like a pincushion—pierced
eyebrows, nose, and lips. I found nothing at all wrong with her appearance. Some of the most spiritual people I have met are tattooed
and pierced all over.

I was thumbing through my Bible looking all spiritual when she
approached me to sit down. She glanced at my Bible, then at me,
then her seat, my Bible again, me, and her seat, while I glanced back
at her, her seat, my Bible, her seat, my Bible, and then her again.
She rolled her eyes. I didn't have pierced anything. And I'm sure she
wasn't impressed with my *Leave It to Beaver* fashion sense. Then she
said, "I'm sitting there. I need to get through." I said, "Yes ma'am,
absolutely, okay, here ya go."

As the plane began to take off, she was thumbing through her CD collection. Rubbing my face as though I was tired and peering through my fingers at her CDs, I noticed she had a CD of the Christian band DC Talk. Like a big dork, I spouted, "You're a Christ-follower?" It scared her. It scared me.

After wiping my spit off her face, she batted her eyelids and said with total annoyance, "Nope, not anymore." *Not anymore?* I thought. "What happened?" I asked. She replied, "Jesus didn't work for me."

Did you catch it? "Jesus didn't work for me." I loved that she was honest, something we Christians fail at miserably. She had stated how many Christians, including myself, live the Christian life: all about me.

Her pursuit of self-satisfaction is normal, though. We are hard-wired with the desire to discover what most satisfies and fulfills us. We settle for what may only last a weekend, a spring break, a night, a summer, or sixty-five years. We miss out on the only One who satisfies our most intense desires. Although overly quoted, C. S. Lewis said it best:

> Our Lord finds our desires not too strong, but too weak. We are half-hearted creatures, fooling about with drink and sex and ambition when infinite joy is offered us, like an ignorant child who wants to go on making mud pies in a slum because he cannot imagine what is meant by the offer of a holiday at the sea. We are far too easily pleased.[1]

Like comparing mud pies in a slum to a holiday at the sea, this girl compared Jesus to something like deodorant, as if Jesus could be traded in for a better brand of Savior. We're no different. We just detour to "self" when Jesus isn't working out. It's called sin—the sin of self. It's our wagging a finger at God, Savior of the world, King of Kings, Lord of Lords, to meet our expectations, our desires, and our standards. Again, my new friend said out loud what almost all people, including Christians, live out every day.

"Okay, God, here's the way it is: it's all about me. I want earth-rattling answers to my prayers, or I won't pray anymore. I'd better hear angels sing when I read the Bible, or I won't read anymore. I'd better feel warm fuzzies at church, or I won't serve anymore. The preacher had better stir me, the people had better approach me and include me, or I won't come anymore. I'd better have a date to the prom this year or be married by age twenty-nine, or I won't obey anymore. I'd better be pain free, comfortable, secure, and happy every day of my life, and my relationship with you had better be fun filled, or I won't follow you anymore."

We're this way with our Creator God. And we're not any better with people. "Hey! Everyone listen up. It's all about me, okay? Laugh loud or weird, and I'll mock you. Get in line in front of me, and I'll curse you. Interrupt my routine, my plans, my weekend, my free time, my nap time, or my to-do list, and I'll jump all over you. Wear clothes that match my taste and celebrity fashion, or I'll avoid you. Talk the way I think you should talk and when I want you to talk, or I'll ignore you. Be quiet and at full attention while I tell you all about my opinion, my pain, my life, or I'll leave you."

Remember the teacher of the law from Mark 12? He agreed with everything Jesus said (vv. 32–33). I mean, he gave the perfect church answer. He recited what he had learned in Sunday school. Then Jesus encouraged him, or perhaps warned him, "You are not far from the kingdom of God" (v. 34). In other words, "Correct answer. But you still didn't get it." Like the teacher of the law, we may think we believe something when actually we are only agreeing. Agreeing rather than believing is the same as not getting it. What we really believe is evident in the way we live.

Jesus said, "Watch out for the teachers of the law. They like to walk around in flowing robes and be greeted in the marketplaces, and have the most important seats in the synagogues and the places of honor at banquets. They devour widows' houses and for a show make lengthy prayers. Such men will be punished most severely" (Mark 12:38–40).

Flaunting their robes, greeted with flattery, front-row seats in the synagogue, red-carpet entrances to the Religious Grammys, and hogging the prayer mic. No doubt "All Eyez on Me" was their iPod's top-rated song.

This reminds me of a story I heard about a class of junior high school girls who would color their lips in three coats of bright red lipstick and then kiss the bathroom mirrors at their school. Lip imprints were all over the mirrors. After several incidents of this bathroom artwork, the custodian, Mr. Smith, was fed up. Refusing to clean the mirrors, he went to the principal and told him he was sick of cleaning lipstick imprints off the girls' bathroom mirror. The principal said, "I've got just the thing."

The principal then began calling groups of girls to the bathroom. When he tried to explain how silly and immature their behavior was, the girls just twirled their hair and stared right through him. He said, "Girls, you are working Mr. Smith to death. Do you even realize how tough it is for him to clean lipstick off these mirrors?" The girls continued daydreaming about the latest sale at the Gap, but the principal went on. "It's really tough on Mr. Smith. As a matter of fact, Mr. Smith, why don't you show these girls how difficult it is for you to clean their lipstick off the mirrors?"

"Sure," answered Mr. Smith. So he took the squeegee he used for cleaning mirrors and windows and walked over to one of the bathroom stalls. He dipped the squeegee in the toilet several times, placed it on the mirror, and began scrubbing as hard as he could.

With their eyes as big as Starbucks Grande coffee mugs, the girls began madly scraping their tongues and scrubbing their lips with their shirtsleeves. A few just had to go lie down. The experience left them all traumatized.[2]

This "me, me, me" attitude that we think will fulfill us and em-power us is the same as kissing all over a "poopy" mirror. It's a love affair with your self that grosses everyone out and eventually leaves a bad taste in your mouth. It offends God at the deepest level. Why? You aren't made for yourself; you are made for God and others.

First John 2:16 speaks of "the cravings of sinful man, the lust of his eyes, and the boasting of what he has and does." This verse actually defines the world. The world is against God, craving, lusting, and boasting in itself, "I am the focus. All eyes off God, all eyes off you, all eyes on *me*! I will seek and pursue whatever pleases me, whatever makes me happy, whatever feels good to me. I will leave no desire unanswered, no impulse unsatisfied, no craving unmet—especially if it brings me empowerment or pleasure."

Enter the trap of self-esteem. We believe self-esteem can be found in whatever makes us seem better than the next guy.

I have self-esteem issues. Everyone has some kind of self-esteem baggage, including beauties like Jessica Simpson. Is low self-esteem such a terrible thing? Yes. But let's think "backward" for a moment. Have you ever considered that the people with the highest self-esteem are in prison for crimes committed against humanity? Think about it. They believed no rules applied to them, nobody mattered but them, and the craving and the lust that lurked in their flesh and before their eyes could not be left unsatisfied—no matter who it hurt, no matter what the law said, and especially no matter what God said.

Oprah's ratings soar and Dr. Phil's fan club grows, evidence of what we believe is most important—improving ourselves, empowering ourselves, and loving ourselves. Yet according to God's holy Word, this is all smoke and poopy mirrors. Jesus says this is life: deny yourself, carry your cross, and follow him (see Luke 9:23). What does that look like? "Love the Lord your God with all your heart. . . . Love your neighbor as yourself" (Mark 12:30–31). Jesus never said the problem was self-esteem; it's God-esteem. Now, don't get me wrong. I like Oprah. I dig Dr. Phil. But I need Jesus. Oprah inspires, Dr. Phil counsels, but Jesus saves and satisfies.

Jesus is totally backward to the world. So let's think backward again, shall we? What if high self-esteem was the curse and low self-esteem was the gift? High self-esteem fuels confidence in ourselves, but low self-esteem propels our need for God. It's like a poet once said: "Intense is the agony—when the eye begins to see, the ear begins to hear, the pulse begins to throb, the heart begins to pound—where the soul feels its flesh, and the flesh feels its chains."[3]

What does low self-esteem do for me? It turns the volume up on my soul's agony—my eyes burn, my ears ring, my pulse races, and my heart pounds at the devastating absolute truth: I'm a slave to self. I'm a slave to emptiness. I'm a slave to *sin*. I need a Savior.

Be honest—feeling any chains yet? Maybe you aren't. Chains of self can somehow make you feel comfortable, secure, free, and "happy," at least for a season. Do you really still believe you just need to "unleash the power within you," or "love yourself more," or "build better self-esteem"? Pucker up, my friend, there's a bathroom mirror with your name on it.

Or is the turmoil awakening in you? Do you feel "These chains are robbing me; that mirror is poisoning me; life is escaping me; sin is killing me"? The bottom line is, I'm in love with me, you're in love with you, and nothing in us can live the way we're meant to live nor love the One we're made for.

We need a Savior.

3

I'm Made for *This?*

We were meant to live for so much more.
Have we lost ourselves?

Switchfoot

I was browsing through the sports section of the *Birmingham News* a while back and read something that made me chuckle. It included a quote from the *Spokane Spokesman-Review*. Coach Mike Holmgren of the Seattle Seahawks pro football team told a reporter how he coached then-rookie kicker Josh Brown: "I say, 'Kick it between the posts.' That's my big coaching point. One day I forgot to tell him that, and he missed one, and I said, 'Josh, I'm here for you—between the posts.'"[1]

Many believers, I think, take the command to "love God and love your neighbor" as a coaching point rather than a command from Jesus. Many seem to feel it's a choice, or maybe a burden, to incorporate it into life or not, based on time and energy. If loving God and others might improve their game, their self, then they're off to work. If it's too tiring, painful, or unrewarding, then it's on to the next drill of self-improvement or self-satisfaction. At best we take Jesus' great commandment as a nice piece of advice to supplement or fit in to all the other yearly goals to help improve our lives. "Meditate, exercise, give to Red Cross, love God and neighbor, get a life coach . . ." At worst, we either ignore the commandment and hog the ball of self-improvement or fire the Coach for an "expert" with a bestselling book.

Jesus doesn't coach improvement for life. He commands fulfillment for life. The problem is, we don't like the word *command*. Whether it is advice, direction, counsel, or a command, we always think we can do better ourselves. We try to love God and other people, on our terms, on our feelings, on our time. But the game of life is in continual overtime. We're drained. We're tired. Still, Jesus commands us to score the goal of loving God with all our DNA and loving others as our selves so that we will find life. But the winning kick is wide right because we love our celebrities more than God, and then wide left because we love our to-do lists more than people. Indeed, loving God and others is why we exist, and why we were created; but it's backward to this world and impossible to live up to. It's ironic to me that Jesus has to command us to do exactly what we're made to do. But the greater irony is that it is impossible. No matter how hard we try we will never be able to keep it between the posts.

Why bother, then? Because there is freedom in doing what we were created and commanded to do—abandoning our lives to God and others. We have deep inside of us a sense that something is just *right* about it. When we accept that we cannot love God and others on our own, we free ourselves from that struggle, allowing God to rip away any dependence on self (or self-help) and expose our desperate need for God-help and God's powerful love. By faith and dependence on God, he fills us, empowers our love for him, and overflows love for others. As the apostle John said, "We love because he first loved us" (1 John 4:19).

The Default of Self-Love

I was in my third semester of graduate school in Louisville, Kentucky. About twice a week I would abandon my eleven-by-fourteen cave and take off to Barnes & Noble to study. Twice a week soon became four times a week after I noticed a cute girl working at the store.

I'd never had the guts to talk to a girl cold turkey. After figuring out her schedule, I would make sure I was there at the same time and sat in the same place—next to the garbage can in the coffee shop. I figured that when she made her rounds through the coffee shop, she would have to throw something away, and I'd have a better chance of meeting her. For weeks she made her rounds, dropping off trash at the garbage can, but of course I was too scared to say anything. It took two weeks before I even had the nerve to look up from my books.

One day as she was throwing used paper coffee cups into the trash, I counted to three and looked up. I nearly choked as I discovered she was looking right at me. This was my shining moment! All I could get out was a shaky "Hi." I even forgot to smile. I had been waiting for that moment for weeks, and I thought I had blown it. But she smiled, returned the "Hi," and slowly walked off as if she was expecting me to say more. But being the mack daddy that I am, I panicked, dropped my head, and pretended to start reading again. I thought to myself, *I'm such a dork.*

A week later I came to a point of no return. All morning I was praying for strength, trying to psych myself up. This was the day that I would reject fear, risk everything, walk right up to her like a love champion, and sweep her off her feet.

Yet during the whole twenty-minute ride to Barnes & Noble, I was praying that she wouldn't be there so I'd have another day to gather my courage. I walked in and took my seat, and there she was at the check-out counter. *No way I'm going to try to talk to her with people around listening to us*, I thought. But then my moment came. Someone took her place behind the register, and she started browsing through the aisles, straightening and rearranging books. "This is it," I whispered. "It's now or never." As quickly as I stood up, my fear rushed back. I found myself darting from aisle to aisle, hiding behind the end of the shelves, working up the strength to meet her. Yeah, there's a name for that—"stalker." Anyway, she passed by, about two rows over. "She's heading back to the register. It must happen now. I must speak to her right now. Okay, take some deep breaths, steady as we go . . ."

I took off walking like a Chihuahua wired on mocha, not really knowing where she had gone. Then I accidentally walked right in front of her, scaring us both half to death. I was caught so off guard that I kept walking. But in that moment of utter disappointment, I stopped, spun around, and shouted, "Excuse me?" I couldn't believe what was happening. The moment was surreal; it was like an out-of-body experience. She turned around, smiled, began walking toward me, and invitingly said, "Yes?" My mind was racing: *Here it is. This is it. This is the moment. What do I say now? I hope I don't say something stupid. Is my zipper up?*

The pressure was more than I could bear. I could tell she was expecting something amazing to roll off my lips—something witty or funny, or perhaps even original. And here I was hyperventilating, with my armpits like faucets and my heart pounding down in my kidneys. I was digging deep for the perfect words to say so she would think I was her knight with shiny forehead who had come to save the day. As we drew close, our eyes locked on one another. Nothing could be heard around us except the melody of Cupid's harp. And in that most gloriously romantic moment, I said, "So you work here, huh?"

That was it. That was the best I could do. That was all I had to offer. It was official: I'm a dork. Her expression went from hoping for a hero to discovering a buffoon. She politely answered, tossed in a couple of extras about herself, and then dropped the finale like a grand piano on my head, "I'd better get back to work."

I stayed a few minutes longer pretending to study so that I wouldn't look humiliated. But the whole time I just wanted to crawl under the table, curl up into the fetal position, suck my thumb, and cry. Finally I got into my car and headed down the interstate. For twenty minutes I shook my head, choked the steering wheel, and repeated over and over to myself in disbelief, "So you work here, huh? So you work here, huh? So you work here, huh?" Good grief.

I got back to my cave of a dorm room and called my dad for sympathy. He obliged. After I got off the phone, I lay down on my bed for a few minutes replaying the drama of all that had happened. I dwelled on every part that I wished I'd done differently. After about ten minutes of sulking, I got up, fixed a bowl of Cheerios, flipped on the TV to *Everybody Loves Raymond*, and carried on with my life. By the time I went to bed that night I had a handful of excuses—why things went wrong, how it was mostly the fault of the bookstore environment or maybe even her fault. I convinced myself that she wasn't that cute, probably had poopy breath, and was stuck up for not seeing that I was a stud, plus I didn't like her as much as I thought I did.

You see, despite the wreck I had made of that situation, I still took care of me, defended myself, and looked out for number one. No problem with loving my "self" here. I'm no different from anyone else. And by the way, in the following two and a half years, I went back to Barnes & Noble maybe three times, and only when I knew she wasn't working. I still looked out for me.

The First Love

What we really need to do is take our eyes off of "me, me, me" and gaze upon the cross. The cross is the key to impossible possibilities. We need Jesus. On the cross God, the God-man, died, and three days later he rose from the grave. Salvation from self and sin was given to us. To put it plainly, through the cross of Jesus Christ we find God's love made public. There we are rescued from sin, death, and the prison of self. At the cross you and I find world-shaking power to live the backward life—the life we are made for.

"We love because he first loved us" (1 John 4:19). The gut truth is this: until you are first loved by God, you have nothing to love with. Let that sink in for a moment: until you are first loved by God, you have nothing to love with. You must first be loved by God and embrace the love of God, or you have no love to give. All the love you have is wrapped around your "self."

You see, it all begins with God. We can't work in, or work out, or work up a love that loves God with all our heart, mind, soul, and strength and loves our neighbor as ourselves. We might try it for a season, or we could fake it. But the truth is, it's impossible—like kicking a 110-yard field goal with a concrete block. Love can only be a work of God. There is no greater demonstration of his love than Jesus' suffering and sacrifice for a world that rejected him. "This is love, *not that we loved God*, but that He loved us and sent His Son to be the [atoning sacrifice] for our sin" (1 John 4:10 NASB, italics mine). It's, therefore, this love of God through Jesus, poured out in us, that propels our hearts to fix themselves upon God and then upon others. "We love because he first loved us" (1 John 4:19).

> This is how God showed his love among us: He sent his one and only Son into the world that we might live through him. This is love: not that we loved God, but that he loved us and sent his Son as an atoning sacrifice for our sins.
>
> 1 John 4:9–10

God is the great lover, the infinite lover, the "backward" lover, the *first* lover! We don't love God; he loves us. We didn't love God; he loved us. The love we have takes; the love God has gives. You never loved God first; you love God because he loved you first.

The "first love" of God pierces your heart, and something stirs within you. It tugs (for some, yanks) your love away from your "self" and toward him. For some this is gradual, for others almost instantaneous. The eyes of your heart are opened, and faith is awakened in your soul. As the love of God grows within you, it becomes active, moving you by faith to embrace his love.

Here's the picture: God says, "I LOVE YOU." Then your eyes behold, your heart breaks, your faith embraces, and you cry, "I love you!"

And the dance begins. It's a love affair with God! It's the love affair you were made for.

Look at the cross. That was God, on a cross . . . for you. Maybe you've been trying everything under the stars to have, buy, and pursue "love," from Internet love connections and dead-end relationships to poker winnings and plastic surgery. Lean in and look at the cross a little closer, and be in awe at the reality that all along God has been chasing you. See, perhaps for the first time, that when there was no love for God in you, there was a heart-breaking, soul-saving, gloriously life-ruining love of God for you.

The Others Love

Living the Christian life means that we embrace the overwhelming love of God and we love God with all our hearts. That would seem enough for life and worship. In fact, I would think that the greatest fulfillment would come only from this vertical relationship with God. But Jesus' words don't stop at love God with all your heart, mind, soul, and strength. He follows with something seemingly distracting from the pursuit of God alone in life and worship—love others. Jesus gave the two commandments and placed them on equal ground. "The most important one . . . 'Love the Lord your God with all your heart. . . .' The second is this: 'Love your neighbor as yourself.' There is no commandment greater than these" (Mark 12:29–31). Notice he said no commandment, not commandments. As backward as it sounds to us, the greatest fulfillment is found in loving God and others.

Love for others is our love relationship with God gone public. Love for others is a public display of affection for God. The evidence that we are loved by God and lovers of God is seen in our love for people. Therefore, I believe that if we have no love for people in our lives, inwardly and outwardly, we have no true love for God, regardless of how spiritual we might speak and act.

Many people (like me) can get pretty good at enjoying the vertical love, the love between them and God. But the part we get spiritual dementia about is the horizontal love—love for others. If you ask me, Christianity would be much easier if not for people. That's why I stress that any possible love for others depends on our love affair with God. Until we are first loved by God, we have nothing to love with. As God's love for us moves and grows our love for him, away from ourselves, it has to spill out and flow out to others. The heart is moved by God's love to have concern for the unloved, compassion for the unlovely, patient and persevering love for the unlovable. God's love for you and your love for God (the love affair) becomes the fuel of your love for others.

Think about all the worship songs and definitions of worship out there today. Worship is often focused on our love affair with God, and rightly so. This is the heart of worship. But worship also has feet—love for others. The backward truth is that worship is not authentic, biblical worship if it only has heart but no feet, or feet but no heart. Jesus established in his greatest commandment that worship has heart ("love God") and feet ("love people").

We'll spend more time on "loving others" later in the book, but I want to get your "feet" planted on God's reality, looking away from self and toward others. You were made to be a giver, not a taker. It's sin and self that direct a life of taking rather than giving. But you and I both know that no matter how much we get, no matter how much we take, we are still never satisfied. Something still seems to be missing. That's because God is a giver, not a taker. And because we were made for God, we too are made to be givers, not takers. And that, my friend, seems flat-out backward to this world of self.

A couple of summers ago, my then-fiancée, Christie, went with me to an airport counter as I checked in for a flight to an event in

Florida. Beside us was a woman sobbing for some unknown reason. As we walked off I turned around to catch one more glimpse of this poor lady. We went over to stand by the wall and prayed for her. After praying, I looked at Christie and said, "I want to go over to that lady and tell her the Lord loves her." So when the right time came, I caught up to her and told her I was a Christ-follower. I said, "My fiancée and I saw you crying, and we just wanted you to know that we prayed for you. I also wanted to tell you that God loves you and will take care of you. Can I pray for you?" Surprisingly, she was very standoffish and did not want me to pray for her. So I told her that Christie and I would be praying for her throughout the rest of the day.

About thirty minutes later, Christie and I were eating burgers at an airport lounge. To our surprise, the woman walked in on the other side and ordered a meal. Christie and I prayed for her again and sensed that God wanted us to pay for her meal. Though we really couldn't afford it, we called the waiter over and told him we wanted to pay for her dinner anonymously. We gave him a note for her telling her that Jesus loved her and that we loved her as well. We asked him not to tell her about the free meal or give her the note until we had left. The waiter was blown away. We gave him a nice tip.

Christie and I walked out of there feeling that Jesus was holding our hands as we held each other's. It was amazing to show love to someone we didn't even know. We powerfully experienced God's presence. We were so joyful and thankful for the chance to serve someone in a sacrificial way. We knew we had experienced "the love for God and others we were made for" Jesus had talked about in the great commandment.

I remember a time when I was on the receiving end of such a radical outpouring of love. I had a Christ-loving friend who wanted, for no apparent reason, to give me a check with a couple extra numbers in the dollars section. It just didn't feel right, although truthfully, I badly wanted to take it from him. So I tried to do what

I thought was the right thing—to be all spiritual and refuse to take it. However, he insisted, even demanded I take it, saying, "Don't steal my joy by not taking this, man!" What do you say to that? So I reluctantly took it.

I walked away with a very uneasy happiness over having taken extra cash to spend on "me." It just didn't sit right. But my friend walked away giddy over sacrificing his meager, hard-earned money on someone else. That is what happens with a love affair with God. You are compelled to serve others.

How I yearn to need people less—need (and want) their money less, need their stuff less, need their applause less, need their acceptance less—and instead love them more. That's what Jesus did. Jesus lived, demonstrated, the life we're made for. How many times have you heard, "God wants to make you more like Jesus"? I finally see why now. It's the greatest fulfillment. And my life's pursuit is to be more like Jesus—loving the God I'm made for, living the life I'm meant for.

It's a backward life—a life of keeping the ball between the posts—a life all about God and all about others, not a life all about us. It's the life we're made for. It's a life that is possible only by God's first love.

4

Will the Real God Please Stand Up?

All my religious beliefs are based on *Star Wars*.

Mike Dirnt, bass player of Green Day

amous rap star Eminem once rapped, "Will the real Slim Shady please stand up?" But I have a close relative who asks, "Will the real God please stand up?" Let me explain. There is a member of my family who is an amazing woman. She is one of the most giving, servant-hearted, intelligent, beautiful women I have known, along with Christie and my own mother. If you were around her, you would think she was one of the godliest women ever. But she is not a follower of Jesus. She loves Jesus to some degree, in that she agrees with his teachings, but she does not believe he is the Savior.

We have had a couple of loving yet challenging conversations about God, Jesus, sin, and Scripture. In one of those conversations, she raised a question that I have never forgotten: "Will the real God please stand up?"

What did she mean by this question? Her explanation was that throughout the ages, cultures have worshiped many different gods. Even today many different religions or beliefs claim their own god or gods to be true. Authentic Christians worship Jesus, Muslims claim Allah, Buddhists seek the "One," and "Madonna has faith on a string" (kabbalah).[1] Moreover, there are movements that combine all of the above to form their own religion or "god."

The world sees Christians wearing crosses around their necks, Christian T-shirts or tattoos on their backs, Jesus bracelets on their wrists, and fish symbols on the bumpers of their Toyotas, and finds it superficial. The world sees many Christians who profess God with their lips but live lives of indifference to God and others. If we Christians really know the one true God, someone once asked me, then why do so many of us deny him with our lives? Is it any wonder a loving woman in my family sincerely asks, "Will the real God please stand up?"

Setting the Stage

We're not the only ones faced with trying to show who the real God is. The prophet Elijah found himself not just in a debate but in the middle of a heavyweight championship showdown between his God and the "god" Baal and his followers. This showdown would have been an HBO pay-per-view headliner for sure, and the fight theme headline on ESPN, in *USA Today*, and in all of the rest of the media would have proclaimed: "Will the Real God Please Stand Up?"

Israel was God's chosen people. Yet Israel shook one fist at God and with the other hand reached out for any other "god" they could find to call their own. As a matter of fact, they were a lot like us. They wanted to serve God on their terms. They even combined worshiping God with the worship of other false "gods," much like many Christians today claim to be a "Buddhist Christian" or believe in Jesus and horoscope predictions. But we don't even have to take it that far—it's also the same as combining worship of God with a lifestyle that is all about "me."

Even though Israel rebelled, replacing God with their idols, God sent prophet after prophet after prophet crying out for them to turn back and serve, worship, and love God alone—the one true God—the one they were made for.

> As surely as I live, declares the Sovereign LORD, I take no pleasure in the death of the wicked, but rather that they turn from their ways and live. Turn! Turn from your evil ways! Why will you die, O house of Israel?
>
> Ezekiel 33:11

But they refused. In fact, they murdered God's prophets one by one as they came along. Elijah felt that he was the only prophet of the Lord left in all of Israel (1 Kings 18:22).

The kings of Israel were most to blame for leading the people away from God. King Ahab, who reigned during Elijah's time, went so far as to set up an altar to the god Baal, and the people fell right in line to worship it. God himself said through Scripture that Ahab did "more to provoke [God] to anger than all the kings of Israel before him" (1 Kings 16:33).

Baal versus Yahweh

Baal and Yahweh (the name of the God of Israel) became an infinitely bigger rivalry than once–heavyweight champions Mike Tyson and Evander Holyfield. God declared through Elijah to King Ahab that he would dam the rains of heaven from falling for the next several years, punishing his rebellious people and proving he was the true God. This was a slap in the face to King Ahab and his god, Baal, who was believed to be the god of rain.

Fast-forward three and a half years and sure enough, it hasn't rained. The people of God still have not turned back to God and away from Baal. Yet God continues to love his people and pursue them. So he takes matters into his own hands. God tells Elijah to book a showdown on Mount Carmel between God and Baal to prove to the people that God alone is the almighty King of glory. Elijah sets off to challenge King Ahab. Ahab sees Elijah in the distance and immediately shouts: "Is that you, you troubler of Israel?" (1 Kings 18:17).

Right out of the dressing room, Ahab has messed up. He's got it all wrong. The rebellion of Israel and Ahab himself against Yahweh is the trouble that is causing the drought, not Elijah. Isn't that just like us, though? We want to believe that the problem is always "out there." We always think that we are the victims. It's like saying, "Drugs almost ruined my life," when actually *I* almost ruined my life . . . with drugs. Once again, it's the "me, me, me" excuse that somebody else was wrong, somebody else caused me to be the way I am or to act the way I did. Plain and simple, it's my environment's fault, it's somebody else's fault. Someone else almost ruined my life. The trouble is "out there." But the trouble, and the problem, is "right here." We are the trouble. We have a problem. We need a Savior.

Back to the story. Elijah is not intimidated by Ahab:

> "I have not made trouble for Israel," Elijah replied. "But you and your father's family have. You have abandoned the LORD's commands and have followed the Baals. Now summon the people from all over Israel to meet me on Mount Carmel. And bring the four hundred and fifty prophets of Baal and the four hundred prophets of Asherah, who eat at Jezebel's [Ahab's wife's] table."
>
> 1 Kings 18:18–19

In other words, "The challenge is on! Meet me at Mount Carmel!" The showdown was beginning:

> So Ahab sent word throughout all Israel and assembled the prophets on Mount Carmel.

Elijah went before the people and said, "How long will you waver between two opinions? If the LORD is God, follow him; but if Baal is God, follow him."

But the people said nothing.

1 Kings 18:20–21

Elijah looked into the eyes of the people and asked, "How long will you 'straddle the fence'?" Actually, the literal words mean, "How long will you limp between two twigs?"

Here's the truth: To serve God and self will cripple your life. To serve God on your terms, at your convenience, when you feel like it, with your own ideas of who or what he is, or combining him with the worship of "me, me, me," or with horoscopes, or Buddha, or whatever, will guarantee journeying through life with a spiritually torn ACL of the knee. It could mean a life apart from God forever. The backward life—the life you were made for—is a marathon journey that you run, not limp through. With God, it's all or nothing:

I know your deeds, that you are neither cold nor hot. I wish you were either one or the other! So, because you are lukewarm—neither hot nor cold—I am about to spit you out of my mouth.

Revelation 3:15–16

We continue the story: now Elijah presents the contract for the showdown. He's outnumbered and outpowered by Ahab and 450 prophets of Baal and 400 prophets of Asherah (850 to 1). Instead of Tyson vs. Holyfield, it is looking more like the Incredible Hulk vs. David Spade. But remember, it's a showdown between Yahweh and Baal, not Elijah and the other prophets.

Then Elijah said to them. . . . "Get two bulls for us. Let them choose one for themselves, and let them cut it into pieces and put it on the wood but not set fire to it. I will prepare the other bull and put it on the wood but not set fire to it. Then you call on the name of your

God, and I will call on the name of the LORD. The god who answers by fire—he is God.

1 Kings 18:22–24

The crowd is gathering now. All bets are final. The lights dim for everyone to take their seats. A guy in a tux enters through the ropes and strides to the middle of the ring. Ding, ding, ding! "LLLLadieees aaand gennntlemen, in the left corner, in the pink robe, is Baal and the land of Phoenicia. And in the right corner, in the robe of glory, is Yahweh and the land of Israel! This will be a two-round fight. Winnnnerrrr taaakkes aaallll!"

Round one begins:

Elijah said to the prophets of Baal, "Choose one of the bulls and prepare it first, since there are so many of you. Call on the name of your God, but do not light the fire." So they took the bull given them and prepared it.

Then they called on the name of Baal from morning till noon. "O Baal, answer us!" they shouted. But there was no response; no one answered. And they danced around the altar they had made.

1 Kings 18:25–26

Picture the scene. For hours and hours these prophets are cheerleading, dancing around, trying to get their god to answer them. It reminds me of self-help. It's like me trying to convince me, empower me, strengthen me to answer me and help me. Yet I call out to me, and no one answers back—not even me, because "me" has the same issues. Follow me?

Yet the self-improvement gurus of our day preach this gospel: "the answer lies inside of you." All you have to do is unleash the champion within. People in their cars listen to the self-help audio books, dancing around the altar of "self," summoning strength and answers from themselves for their life's fears, failures, emptiness, and pain. But just like the prophets calling out to Baal, there is no answer, nor will there ever be one.

Elijah gave the Baal prophets the terms of the challenge in the morning. Then it's as if he got himself a Red Bull and a bag of Doritos and kicked back in his lawn chair to enjoy the show. He even started talking "smack" to them (kind of a "naaa-naaa-na-boooboo"): "At noon Elijah began to taunt them" (1 Kings 18:27). Elijah had watched these prophets try to get Baal to show up all day, and he couldn't hold it in any longer. He leaned forward in his chair, cleared his throat, cupped his hands around his mouth, and barked:

> "Shout louder! . . . Surely he is a god!" . . . So they shouted louder and slashed themselves with swords and spears, as was their custom, until their blood flowed. Midday passed, and they continued their frantic prophesying until the time for the evening sacrifice. But there was no response, no one answered, no one paid attention.
>
> 1 Kings 18:27–29

I understand what it means to be taunted. I played college basketball, and during my redshirt year at Samford University, I was sitting on the bench while we were getting pummeled by Davidson. Their lead was up to 25 points. Some students directly behind me were yelling, "Hey, number 45! Maybe they'll let you play a little now that we're kicking your $#%&!"

Then Davidson got up to a nearly 40-point lead. Well, that just sent the students mocking me into an absolute frenzy. They were like a verbal swarm of bees; I was amazed at all the chants they came up with not just about us but about me! Here's my favorite: "Number 45, we're up by 40 and your coach still won't let you play? You must really suck!"

Great memories.

Seriously, I've been mocked by opponents and even crowds before. It's not fun. The more they taunted and the more it got to me, the angrier and "dumber" I became. I'd miss a shot, or I'd get taken out of the game and yell out at the air, kick chairs, and slam my water bottle to the floor—and eventually foul out of the game. That's how it was when Elijah was jeering at these prophets and it was getting to them. But instead of kicking chairs, they "shouted louder and slashed themselves with swords and spears, as was their custom, until their blood flowed" (v. 28).

Elijah has no mercy on these false prophets. He knows Yahweh will mop the mountain floor with Baal. He harps, "Perhaps he [Baal] is deep in thought, or busy [literally "relieving himself"], or traveling. Maybe he is sleeping and must be awakened" (v. 27). Elijah is pouring it on with no mercy! "Yo, prophets! I think I know what's wrong. Baal is on the toilet, deep in thought, catching up on the latest issue of *Reader's Digest*. Or maybe he got an Internet deal on an Alaskan cruise and is gone for a month. Or he might have dozed off in his recliner watching *Seinfeld* reruns." Elijah is making his point: Baal does not exist; Baal will not answer; Baal is a lie.

We have our own "Baals" today—palm readers, psychics, superstitions, horoscopes, and so forth. I was in a bookstore the other day enjoying a cup of coffee and thumbing through some poetry. For the life of me, I absolutely cannot get poetry! It frustrates the heck out of me! I avoid it like the plague now, unless it begins "Roses are red, violets are blue . . ." But I digress.

I enjoy walking around and looking over the empty tables to see what books people have been browsing through. That day my eye caught a little book called *Feng Shui: Do's and Taboos*. Feng shui, according to the author, is "one of the five components that determine one's destiny." The book is basically a how-to guide to channeling the "energies" of life to bring a person "success, fun and good fortune." The author advises us to "keep the seats, covers, and doors to the bathrooms shut at all times, especially if the toilet faces a bedroom or directly faces the bathroom door, because toilets emanate negative energy."[2]

Toilets do give off something negative after people are done in the bathroom, but I wouldn't call it "energy." Notice also the fine print on the copyright page. The disclaimer states, "All recommendations are made without guarantee. . . . The author and publisher disclaim any liability in connection with the use of this information."³ I don't want to go "Elijah" on this author. Let me just say that my point is the same as Elijah's: feng shui does not have power; horoscopes do not answer; they just aren't true.

Intermission: Elijah has enjoyed the ridiculousness of the Baal prophets about as much as I enjoy the hoopla over the latest celebrity scandals or breakups. In other words, it's interesting for a while, but then it gets just plain old and annoying. Elijah got back to work.

> Then Elijah said to all the people, "Come here to me." They came to him, and he repaired the altar of the Lord, which was in ruins. Elijah took twelve stones, one for each of the tribes descended from Jacob, to whom the word of the Lord had come, saying, "Your name shall be Israel."
>
> 1 Kings 18:30–31

The time had come for the real God to stand up. "Gather 'round, gather 'round," Elijah called out. God's people had been watching the carnival of the Baal prophets all day long. Realizing it was a fake, they drew near to hear the Word of God and witness his power. This is what we too need to do—realize the hopelessness of self, "empty religion," horoscopes, and superstitions, and instead be drawn near to hear the Word and to see the power of the one true God of the universe. Draw near to him, and he will draw near to you (see James 4:8), and he will put the stones of your life and the altar of your heart back together again, just as "with the stones [Elijah] built an altar in the name of the Lord" (1 Kings 18:32).

And then round two began:

> With the stones he built an altar in the name of the Lord, and he dug a trench around it large enough to hold two seahs of seed. He arranged the wood, cut the bull into pieces and laid it on the wood. Then he said to them, "Fill four large jars with water and pour it on the offering and on the wood."
>
> "Do it again," he said, and they did it again.

"Do it a third time," he ordered, and they did it the third time. The water ran down around the altar and even filled the trench.

1 Kings 18:32–35

Three times the altar, the meat, and the wood were soaked with water! We are talking about twelve barrels of water! The ditch was also filled to the brim. Elijah wanted everyone to know that he wasn't going to pull a proverbial "rabbit out of the hat" magic trick and set it all on fire. I remember bringing firewood into our home for the fireplace as a kid. Let me tell you, soaked wood doesn't even smolder, much less burn.

You gotta see what Elijah did next. He didn't do a dance, he didn't reach within himself to "unleash the power within," and he didn't say "Roses are red, violets are blue, Baal's on the toilet . . ." He simply drew near to his God.

> At the time of the sacrifice, the prophet Elijah stepped forward and prayed: "O LORD, God of Abraham, Isaac and Israel, let it be known today that you are God in Israel and that I am your servant and have done all these things at your command. Answer me, O LORD, answer me, so these people will know that you, O LORD, are God, and that you are turning their hearts back again."

1 Kings 18:36–37

Power will not come from within. Power will not come from spiritual yoga and meditation, tapping into positive "energies" of the yin/yang, or seeking "the Force" from *Star Wars*. Power comes from stepping into the presence of the one true God through prayer. Yet there is something more here. Did you catch the guts of Elijah's prayer? What did he express twice in his prayer? That it would be known that the Lord (Yahweh) is God. Elijah declared the name and celebrity of God—the One we're made for—above all else, even himself. That's backward to what we know in this world. It puts the source of power where it belongs—in God. It's how we take God's love public, turning the hearts of his people back again. It's pursuing life and doing life backward.

The words have barely left Elijah's lips when God explodes a thunder jolt and firebolt from the heavens, devouring not just the wood and the meat but the rocks, the water in the ditch, and even the dirt!

> Then the fire of the LORD fell and burned up the sacrifice, the wood, the stones and the soil, and also licked up the water in the trench.
>
> 1 Kings 18:38

Knockout! With one blow, Baal was crushed, finished, done, gone, bye-bye, just like the altar. Yahweh forever was, is, and shall be the eternal heavyweight champion of the universe.

God's people were awed beyond human comprehension, no doubt looking like deer caught in headlights: gulping, batting their eyelids, afraid to move a finger, unable to make sense of what had just happened before their very eyes. So what did they do? They fell flat on their faces and worshiped with all their might.

> When the people saw this, they fell prostrate and cried, "The LORD— he is God! The LORD—he is God!"
>
> 1 Kings 18:39

Those words mean colossally more than our feeble "You da man! You da man!" These people literally cried out, "Yahweh—he is the God! Yahweh—he is the God!"

God: The Backward Hero

Did you notice that nobody ran up to get Elijah's autograph? No movie producers, publicists, book agents, or reporters from *Christianity Today* and Fox News hounded him. No one approached him to be that year's Dove Awards host either. God was the hero that day, not Elijah. God is always the hero. The only reason the people of God ever turned back to him was because God himself turned their hearts back through his Spirit and power. God is the hero of every book and every story of the Old Testament—not Moses, not Noah, not Samson, not King David, and not Elijah. God is always the hero.

God doesn't rain fire from heaven upon animal altars anymore. But many, many years later, God did more than stand up: he showed up, and he hung up, and he gave himself up . . . on a cross. God, in the form of his Son Jesus, did something more powerful than words can express. God the Son, Jesus, stepped out of heaven and laid himself on the altar of the cross for our sin and rebellion. He took on the holy, fiery wrath of God the Father. Then, three days later, he walked out of a grave so that all the heavens would proclaim, "He is God! He is God!" God was then, and still is today, the hero.

> All together now—applause for God! Sing songs to the tune of his glory, set glory to the rhythms of his praise. Say of God, "We've never seen anything like him!" When your enemies see you in action, they slink off like scolded dogs. The whole earth falls to its knees—it worships you, sings to you, can't stop enjoying your name and fame.
>
> Psalm 66:1–4 Message

"Will the real God please stand up?" My friend, behold your God.

5

How Big Is Your Daddy?

You're a god and I am not.

Vertical Horizon,
"You're a God"

I'm told I'm a big guy. Six-foot-seven, about 240 pounds (and climbing), to be exact. I get a lot of stares and comments, especially from little kids. A time or two while at a restaurant salad bar I've had little boys walk up, stand right under me, and stare. "What's up, little man?" I ask. The kid, still staring, says, "Wow, you're big!" "Froot Loops did this to me," I say. Usually that'll get a chuckle and a high five, and another lifetime devotee of Froot Loops is born.

One time, though, a chuckle turned to a snarl. Instead of giving me a high five, the boy put his hands on his hips and declared, "Well, my daddy's bigger than you!"

So you know what I tell these kids now? I squat down, eyeball-to-eyeball with them, smile, point toward the sky, and say, "Oh yeah? Well, my 'Daddy'? My Daddy's bigger than the whooole world."

Who's Your Daddy?

Once again, the world has it wrong. We downsize God into an image we can understand, labeling him "a higher power," "the man upstairs," "my copilot," or "the big guy in the sky."

A while back, as I was preparing a PowerPoint display for an upcoming message, I came across a website that had a cartoon picture of the earth. Standing on top was a tiny cartoon god dressed like a leprechaun, with big ears, a white beard, and a cheesy smile, waving hello. That's the world's and perhaps some Christians' view of God. No wonder many Christians struggle in their faith. No wonder many of their lives are powerless and self-centered. No wonder it's easy to point fingers at God when the bad times roll.

A cartoon god is not the God of the backward life. It's not the God of the Bible, nor the God of Elijah. God is backward to our human understanding.

In the book of Romans, Paul is "honking off" about the wonder of this God. In Romans 6, he boasts that God's gift is life forever (v. 23). In Romans 7, he stares down the barrel of sin and "self," yet cries, "Thanks be to God, Jesus Christ will rescue me" (v. 25, my paraphrase).

In Romans 8, Paul is dazzled by the truth that "all things work together for the good of those who love God and are called according to his purpose" (v. 28, my paraphrase). In Romans 9:18, Paul trembles at the mystery that "God has mercy on whom he wants to have mercy, and hardens whom he wants to harden."

In Romans 10, he's overcome with the knowledge that God saves all who believe in their hearts that God raised Jesus Christ from the dead (v. 9). Then, in Romans 11, it's as if Paul hits this moment where all of the truths of God become more than he can bear. Tears fill his eyes, and he takes a deep breath, throws his arms up into the air, fixes his eyes on heaven, and cries out:

Oh, the depth of the riches of the wisdom and knowledge of God! How unsearchable his judgments, and his paths beyond tracing out!

Who has known the mind of the Lord? Or who has been his counselor? Who has ever given to God, that God should repay him? For from him and through him and to him are all things. To him be the glory forever! Amen.

Romans 11:33–36

Translation: "My Daddy's bigger than the whole world!" How big is your Daddy?

Father's Ways

Paul is reaching for words to express the greatness of his God. "Oh, the depth of the riches of the wisdom and knowledge of God! How unsearchable his judgments, and his paths beyond tracing out!" (Rom. 11:33).

God's wisdom: his knowing the best for all things. God's knowledge: his knowing all things. God's judgments: his purpose for all things. God's paths: his ways of accomplishing his purpose for all things.

I love echoes. You stand above a water well and yell, "I love buffalo wings," you get "I love buffalo wings" right back. You stand on the top of a mountain and yell, "Scrumptralescent," you get "Scrumptralescent." You stand at the threshold of the canyon of God's rich wisdom and knowledge and yell, "Ricola," you get . . . silence. You don't get an echo, because the riches of God's wisdom and knowledge are bottomless, infinite, forever, eternal, never ending.

God is not just bottomless in wisdom and knowledge; he is rich in wisdom and knowledge. We're not talking about a spare-change, on-sale, half-off, Christmas clearance wisdom and knowledge of God. We are talking about the heavens-cannot-contain-him, universal-Swiss-bank-accounts-don't-even-compare kind of wisdom and knowledge of God. If wisdom is needed, why waste time at the ATM of self-help when you can go straight to the treasury mint of

God himself, "who gives [wisdom] generously to all without finding fault" (James 1:5).

God's judgments are unsearchable, and his "paths beyond tracing out." Trying to search out God's purposes for tsunamis, and his only way of salvation through Christ alone, is like seeking to understand where God came from or why Keanu Reeves is a movie star. Human logic cannot explain God, his purposes, or his ways of accomplishing his purposes.

Earlier this year I was speaking at a camp and was approached by a college-aged girl and her boyfriend. Looking for logical explanations to the mystery of God and his ways, she peppered me with thought-provoking questions. They were excellent questions. I truly didn't want to cop out and just say, "It's a mystery. The secret things belong to God" (Deut. 29:29). But that was as far as I could go. Color me a wimp, I don't mind. I'm okay with the fact that I don't have all the answers. Trying to answer her questions about God with logical answers would be like my Chihuahua trying to logically explain me.

If you could gather all of God's knowledge, wisdom, judgments, and paths together, you'd get the glory of God's established existence. You'd know his decisions and the choices he makes concerning his all-controlling rule. Ultimately you'd understand his plan of saving humankind. This God goes beyond the outer limits of our imagination. He even has to talk to us in simple sentences, like we talk to babies when we play with them or teach them to speak. The Bible is God's "gaa-gaa, goo-goo" baby talk to us to help us understand him more. This merely gives us "peephole access"—a little glimpse—into his vast ways and thoughts.

Daddy Knows Best

God knows what is best for all things. My son, Josiah, screams and cries while getting a vaccination shot. But his daddy knows that what hurts for a moment keeps him safe from disease and life-threatening illness. Daddy knows best. And so does our Father God.

Even in the details, God knows all things. He knows every little stubble and strand of hair on my head, what I'll eat for lunch tomorrow, and what dress my great-great-great-granddaughter will wear to her prom.

God will accomplish his purpose for all things. His purpose and ways are unsearchable and cannot be traced out. His ways are not our ways (Isa. 55:8). Think about it: God on a cross saving people who hate him? How do you explain that? Or me, a small-town, southern-born, southern-bred Alabama boy meeting my wife in Connecticut—what's up with that? We take so many of these things for granted, but when you stop long enough to think about it, you see that many of the things that happen in our lives are unexplainable.

My summers are usually booked six to nine months in advance with speaking engagements. But for the summer I met my future bride, I had little booked by January. My friend Craig, from Connecticut, had just started a young adult gathering called CORE and asked me to consider being the speaker for it that summer. I considered it over the following weeks and felt it was the right thing to do. A blank summer and this opportunity just pops up?

I moved to New Milford, Connecticut, for the summer. I turned thirty years old the first Sunday I was there, bummed about still being single. I was never one of those superspiritual guys who wanted to stay single until I was thirty years old so I could grow nearer to the heart of God in preparation for my wife. No way. I wanted an instant wife. I will confess that years earlier I'd made out a list of all the qualities I wanted in a wife. My list included the following: Christian, athletic, five-foot-six, funny, easygoing, loves movies. Well, many single years later I tossed the list and prayed, "Lord, I'll just take a Christian woman with a tooth."

At age thirty with no future bride in sight, I thought about Jesus, who was thirty and single when he was baptized by John the Baptist. So I asked my friend Craig to baptize me in his parents' pool to imitate this same point in Jesus' life. The holy moment fell flat when I came out of the freezing water hyperventilating, choking Craig, and grabbing at the air trying to breathe. After taking some deep breaths, regaining my composure, and dismissing Craig, I lifted my hands to heaven and confessed my "bummed-ness" to God. I complained to God, "Why do you still have me single?" Then I prayed, "If you want me to be single, then okay, I guess. But I pray so hard, Lord, that you would change my desires and give me the desire to be single if that is truly what you want. Lord, I so want to meet the love of my life!"

The very next day, at 3:45 and 33.7 seconds p.m., she walked into the room.

It was the first time I was to meet all of the leadership of CORE. Christie and her roommate were tired to the bone from a church small group party they had hosted the night before and had decided they weren't going to this meeting. Christie had every reason not to go. On top of everything else, she still had people from out of town at her house. But Christie's roommate persuaded her to go. She really felt Christie ought to attend the meeting but wasn't sure why.

Christie arrived about fifteen minutes late. I nearly "fumbled my cookies," she was so beautiful. At a midmeeting break I "stalked" her (I seemed to stalk a lot), we talked, and the rest is history. I remember asking her on our first date what her favorite thing about God was. She answered, "His grace." I almost dropped on one knee and proposed right there on the sidewalk. We were married one year and twenty-five days later.

I had tried for years to find "the one." Yet in God's timing and by God's purpose, he personally took me to the one, my wife—in Connecticut! Oh, and did I mention that she had saved for a year to move to New York City that summer but it had fallen through? (And by the way, I don't believe in that talk going around that says God will bring you "the one" when he becomes your complete desire. If that were the case, Christians would have to be celibate. We never want God completely. Well, maybe during the worship song at the conference, we might. But God doesn't wait until we're ready. He waits until he's ready, which is ultimately the very best timing for us too.)

After Christie and I were married, we wanted kids immediately. But since our engagement had been long distance and our finances were low, we decided to wait for a couple of years to have children. Christie was on birth control. But God was moving in our hearts about the timing of having children. We told the Lord we didn't know any better than to spend the first couple of years growing in love and grace together in our marriage. At the same time, we prayed for God to do away with man's device of birth control and grant us a child if it was his will. Eight months later, guess what?

Christie said to me the week of Valentine's Day, "Jarrod, I think I'm pregnant." I responded, "Baby, there is no way you are pregnant. Aren't birth control pills 99.999 percent effective? You aren't pregnant." Then she said, "Can we just stop and get a pregnancy test?" "Chris," I sympathetically answered, "let's not, and go eat buffalo wings instead."

It was Valentine's week, and I was leaving to speak at a weekend youth event through Valentine's Day in Missouri. The Thursday before I left, she walked in the door from work and said, "Jarrod, can you come and sit down for a minute?" "Sure," I remarked with glee, thinking she had a big pre-Valentine's Day surprise gift for me. I had no idea what was in store. She pulled out the "tester." At lunch that day she had purchased the pregnancy test, took it, and *voilà*—pregnant! She handed the stick to me. I had no clue what I was looking at. But I knew she had to be showing this to me for a reason. I got up, walked around the room with my mouth wide open, and kept saying, "It can't be! It can't be!" Well, it was, and he now is!

We went to the pregnancy doctor, whatever he's called. Walking through the hallways, going to different rooms, seeing all those pregnant women, well, I was a bit traumatized by the experience, but I hung in there.

We went into a room where a lady with blue pants rubbed "stuff" on Christie's belly, 10W30, I think. Then she placed the thingy on her stomach. Unbelievably, we saw this little blob . . . with a heartbeat! We could even hear the heartbeat! I just stood there in utter awe. I blurted out, "Is it a girl or a boy?" It was only a blob, for goodness' sake.

A Yankee wife (I mean that affectionately), a child on the way within eight months of marriage, and a bank account with more cobwebs than cash . . . it's not the way I would have done it, nor have expected it. But God is always backward to my ways, my plans.

Father's Power

Back to Paul's question: "Who has known the mind of the Lord? Or who has been his counselor?" (Rom. 11:34).

Answer: nobody! Although many think they have God against the ropes and figured out—"A loving God wouldn't do this. . . . A loving God wouldn't allow that. . . ."—that's human talk. God says, "I am God. You are not."

> "For my thoughts are not your thoughts, neither are your ways my ways," declares the LORD. "As the heavens are higher than the earth, so are my ways higher than your ways and my thoughts than your thoughts."
>
> Isaiah 55:8–9

Nevertheless, many refuse to believe that God is who and what he says he is. You can trust that he will do what he says he will do. Not in our time but in his. Not in our ways but his. Not according to our plan but his. He is God, and we are not. It's simply backward to us. If I had been able to have things my way, I'd have opted out of the devastation of a post-college girlfriend leaving me for another man. I would rather have had God get and keep my attention when I was nine years old, singing the last verse of "Amazing Grace" at church, instead of years later. But his thoughts and ways are not mine, nor yours.

Oh, by the way, in case you've ever wondered—God doesn't need you. And he doesn't need me. He doesn't need job training, law school, Bible college, or Dr. Phil. "Come on!" Paul is saying. "Who has ever had God lie on the sofa for psychotherapy?" God needs nothing and no one. He's not depressed or confused. He doesn't need direction or advice. God didn't sneak into my room at 3:30 this morning or any other morning and say, "Hey, Jarrod, how can I make celebrity marriages work? What am I going to do about the Middle East?"

Paul's still bringin' the heat: "Who has ever given to God, that God should repay him?" (Rom. 11:35). He's not pulling these truths out of the air. Paul has read his Old Testament: "Whom did the Lord consult to enlighten him, and who taught him the right way? Who was it that taught him knowledge or showed him the path of understanding?" (Isa. 40:14).

Giving to God that God might repay implies that God is needy. God didn't create people because he was needy or lonely. Indeed, from him, through him, and to him are all things. So then it begs the question, if God didn't create us because he needed us or because he was lonely, why are we here? Why do you and I exist? We exist for God. We are made for God. He made us for the ultimate—to know him, enjoy him, be loved by him, and love him, forever. We are to keep our focus on him, not on ourselves. We are to serve him out of a love that cannot be contained. As John says, "We love because he first loved us" (1 John 4:19).

Now, if God doesn't need us and we're not here because he is lonely, why does he demand so much from us?

God calls us to the great commandment and demands so much from us because he knows that he alone is the most perfect, the most beautiful, the most powerful, the most satisfying Being in all existence. He is the great lover God whose love is better than life (Ps. 63:3) and in whose presence is the fullness of joy and pleasures forever (Ps. 16:11). You are made for him. Complete satisfaction and joy can only be found in him and in obedience to his commands.

Why then would he not command us to the greatest, most satisfying pursuit in all of life—loving him?

So what does this mean? It means that the Bible is not what so many people take it to be—a bunch of do's and don'ts that rip our "fun" away. First of all, it's backward that he has to tell us to do what we are made for—to love and serve him and others! Second, his commands are not rules that make our lives a bore but rather the desires of a divine Lover wooing us to him and all the satisfaction of true life.

When you serve God and others, don't wait for a "thank you" from God, either. You could never stack enough "favors" up into the cosmos to equal what God has done for you. "For from him and through him and to him are all things. To him be the glory forever! Amen" (Rom. 11:36).

All that you could ever do for him is done because of him and through him. Until he first loved you, you couldn't offer him a thing. You were focused on self. The greatest truth is this: You don't have to break your back with favors to reach God. You can't do enough good works to make up for all the things you've done wrong. God first reached out for you and claimed you back to himself by breaking himself, in the form of his Son, so that you might know his love and his glory. It's called grace.

God-Father

How big is your Daddy? If you're not a Christian, can I be upfront with you? Without Jesus, you're an orphan without the Father you're made for.

If you are a Christian, can I be blunt with you? The reason you struggle with sin—bitterness, anger, worry, fear, jealousy—is because you made your Daddy smaller than he is. Belief in a cartoon-sized God works about a thimbleful of power in your life. When that's the case, the idol of self (as well as circumstances, moods, etc.) will continue to control you. Very simply, your "daddy" is the idol of self you created—instead of the infinite God-Father who created you.

Backward Father

God's infinite ways and thoughts are impossible to fully understand. But greater understanding is possible. Think backward. . . .

WORLD: Say, God, look at creation! You made a world, and it's a mess. It's broken.

GOD: I love you, world. I love you so much that I will give my only Son so that you might live forever.

WORLD: You're looking for a nation to call your own, God? Well, check out Babylon. They've got more gold than they know what to do with. And take a look at those armies. Have you even tried to count all their people? And ooooh, the women! Marry for the money, God!

GOD: See that little nation over there? Yeah, that little forgotten nation with a few scattered people, over in the corner, dressed in rags. . . . Yeah, that's right—Israel. They're mine!

WORLD: Okay, Joshua, if you want to conquer Jericho, listen close. Get on the horn and call in the Navy Seals to scope it out. Then follow up with a bombing campaign to shock and awe them to despair. Then send the tanks and troops in through the gates and take them out.

GOD: Joshua, gather my people and march around the city for seven days. On the seventh day I want all of you to march around the city seven times, and on the seventh lap, I want you to stop, sound the trumpets, and shout with all your might to the glory of my name! Then the walls will fall, and the city will be yours.

WORLD: What's that? God's Son has been born here? Hey, where's my intern? There you are, Billy—listen up. God's Son is here. Call the pope and put him on standby. Contact Fox News, CNN, and the networks and make the announcement. Get the webpage ready. And don't forget to call Hollywood—we're going to make him a star!

GOD: Today my Son, the Savior, is born. And you'll find him in a cave with donkeys, wrapped in rags and lying in a feeding trough.

WORLD: (thirty years later): Has anyone seen Jesus? We've called all the churches, the resorts, the pope, the world leaders, and the Christian Broadcasting Network. No one can find him! Anyway, get the limo and the bulletproof glass ready. When the people are lined up for the parade, get the pope and Jesus in the limo, behind the glass, waving to all their fans.

GOD: I love you so much it hurts (with his one hand wiping away the tears of a homeless, HIV-infected lady, with his other arm around a bunkmate at the shelter, the town crack addict).

WORLD: Love? You want to know love? Love is diamonds! Diamonds are forever.

GOD: Love? You want to know love? Love is a cross and life forever.

WORLD: Life? Life is looking out for number one—me. It's all about me. Whatever makes me happy, comfortable, and secure. You do your thing; I'll do mine. It's all relative. As long as it doesn't bother me, I don't care what you do. It's your life—who cares?

GOD: Life? Life is denying yourself, carrying your cross, and following me.

So how big is your daddy? My daddy? My Daddy's backward to the whole world!

6

Gloriously Ruined

If a human being lives a good life ... an all-just and all-merciful God is going to set the guy on fire for eternity? I don't think so.

Bill O'Reilly, *Who's Looking Out for You?*

I never had a steady girlfriend during my high school and college years. Don't get me wrong; I wasn't a monk. I hung out with girls and went out on dates, but I never had a steady girlfriend. I was basically too in love with "me" and too married to basketball.

Upon graduating from college, I was ready to meet "the one." You know what I mean by "the one," don't you? We always think that if everything else fails, meeting and marrying "the one" will ultimately satisfy our souls.

I met her on a spring break. By about a year later, I was in a serious relationship with her. I remember telling my sister when I was a teenager that the first girl I ever told "I love you" would be my wife. Within six months of dating this girl, my "I love you's" were flowing like curse words at an Alabama versus Auburn football game.

Hit the fast-forward button to two years later. I was within a week of asking her to marry me. I was in business at the time and had just returned home from a business trip. I called her to ask if we were staying at her place or mine for the weekend. Her response was, "Jarrod, I never want to see you again."

"What?" I asked. "Could you put my girlfriend back on the phone? I can't be talking to the same person."

"It's over, Jarrod," she said. "I don't want to be with you anymore."

I was paralyzed. My life was crumbling all around me. "Please don't leave me. *Please!* I'll do anything, but please, please, don't leave me!" I sobbed.

"I'm sorry, Jarrod," she whispered.

"Is there someone else?" I asked, clinching my eyes, biting my lip, and holding my breath. She paused and then dropped the bomb: "Yes, there's someone else," she answered. Fade to black—the lights went out in my world.

I hung up the phone feeling that my soul had been ripped in two. I called my mother on the phone as I jetted down the interstate. "Come home, Jarrod. Please, son, just come home," she begged.

"No, Mom. I gotta handle this somehow."

After one week of trying to "handle it like a man" (which didn't work for me), I came to the end of myself. I went into my bedroom one night, closed the door, turned off the lights, fell onto my knees, then onto my face, and lay as flat as I could on the floor. I couldn't get low enough before my God. Burying my face into the carpet and grabbing fistfuls of it, I screamed and cried out to God: "*Jesus! Help me!* I can't get low enough! I can't get low enough, Lord. Oh, God, I'm so sorry for having flipped you off all of my life. Jesus, I need you."

In that moment, something happened. God peeled back the curtain, and I caught a glimpse of his holiness. And for an instant, things actually got worse for me.

Under the glorious light of that holiness, I no longer felt the pain of loss, but much worse—I saw the horror of my sin. I thought I'd be crushed by it. A second brokenness ensued. For the first time in my life, even though I had heard about it all my life, Jesus on the cross became crystal clear. God was "holy, holy, holy," and I was a "sinner, sinner, sinner." Without Jesus, I was a dead man. Jesus, God the Son, hung on a cross and made the way to his holy Father possible. Through my repentance (confessing and turning from my sin) and faith, Jesus took the hand of his holy Father and my hand and brought them together. In that moment, not only did the lights flicker back on in my world but the Son dawned in my soul. Brokenness first brought me to God, and then God brought a life-changing, mind-bending brokenness to me. That night, on the carpet of my apartment bedroom, God gloriously ruined my life.

Who Is This God?

When I finally met the woman who would become my wife, I drooled all over myself because her beauty stunned me. But I wanted to know more than her beauty. I wanted to know who she really was—what made her giddy, what made her cringe, what made her angry. I wanted to know the real "her," because knowing the real "her" would affect how I talked to her, how I treated her, how I served her, how I loved her.

In the same way, it is not enough to know that God exists or that he is the one true God—nor is it all that he wants us to know. We must know the real "him" because it shapes how we serve him, love him, and worship him and how we view and do life. Indeed, not knowing the true God could cost you your soul.

So buckle up. God is not just love, but he's devastatingly holy. I bet God is backward to everything you've known. He's not just a God who loves but a holy God who ruins—gloriously ruins.

Brokenness

In the year that King Uzziah died . . .

Isaiah 6:1

As Isaiah chapter 6 begins, the lights have just gone out in Isaiah's world. Isaiah believed that God was going to use his king, King Uzziah, to bring revival to the spoiled brats of Israel. Bringing about changes that pleased God, Uzziah had been a godly king of Israel until he disrespected God by arrogantly rushing into the Holy of Holies of God's temple. Struck with leprosy, King Uzziah went into isolation, and things began to slip. Isaiah still had hope in what God might do through him, until he got the news Uzziah had died. Brokenness invaded Isaiah's world.

Let's pause for a second here. Can I get personal for a moment? Are you tasting any brokenness right now, wondering if the sun will ever shine again in your world? Maybe your husband said, "There's someone else," or your girlfriend wrote, "I don't want to see you anymore," or your parents' twenty-year marriage ended with a slammed door and "It's over," or you got the memo reading "regretfully" and "terminated," or your doctor confirmed "It's cancer," or a policeman delivered the soul-quaking news "There's been an accident . . . I'm so sorry."

Brokenness comes in many forms and levels. It can leave hope in ruins at our feet. When darkness surrounds us, we will turn to anything to make sense of it all, to find relief in our pain, to find comfort in our sorrow, to find something we can grab ahold of.

For some strange reason, we often turn inward, to ourselves. Instead of crying out to God, we point the finger at God. Isn't it strange how we lose ourselves in music, the Internet, golf, Texas hold 'em, food, friends, sitcoms, talk shows, work, or our parents? Sorrow turns to anger and bitterness or Jack Daniels and Marlboro Lights. What did Isaiah do when his hope was splintered? He ran to God. It seems the last place we turn is to God. Yet the times of brokenness and despair are where we will see God.

I had a seminary professor whose brother had been diagnosed with cancer. His brother was also a pastor. The pastor had turned inward, filled with anger and bitterness. He sank into deep depression over his disease. A year later my professor visited his brother, the pastor, and found a new man. My professor asked, "What has happened? What has changed?" His brother answered, "God gave me a new vision of himself."

That's what brokenness did for me, and it is exactly what brokenness can do for all of us who surrender ourselves to him. Brokenness brings you to the breaking point where you have nowhere to look but up. There you behold the eyes of the One who is sovereign (in control of all things), glorious, and holy.

Mine Eyes Have Seen the Glory

I saw the Lord seated on a throne, high and exalted. . . .

Isaiah 6:1

There Isaiah stands in silence, eyes widening, heart pounding, beholding his God on the throne. He didn't see an "Out to lunch—back in one hour" sign on the throne. Isaiah didn't see God running back to the throne. He didn't see God running around the throne putting a team together to figure out how to find Osama Bin Laden. God was sitting on the throne in complete control, not saying "Uh-oh" or asking "What happened?" or wondering "What now?" As he was then, he is today, in control of his good and perfect plan. Remember the cone-shaped top that you would put on the table and spin with your fingers? Often our lives seem to be spinning out of control, but in reality our lives are spinning in the palm of God's hand.

And the train of his robe filled the temple.

Isaiah 6:1

Isaiah didn't say that God filled the temple or that God's robe filled the temple. He said that only the *train* of God's robe filled the temple! If just the train of God's robe is this colossal, can you imagine the God who is wearing the robe?

I can picture my wife's wedding gown on our wedding day. It was simple but striking. Her gown didn't have a long train. I've been to some weddings where the bride rounds the corner of the church doors and the train of her dress keeps going and going and going, like a grand slam at Boston's Fenway Stadium.

Think of just the train of God's robe of glory filling and covering the universe like a blanket, draping over the moon, the stars, the planets, and the galaxies.[1]

> Above him were seraphs, each with six wings: With two wings they covered their faces, with two they covered their feet, and with two they were flying.
>
> Isaiah 6:2

Isaiah is awed by the seraphs (angels) flying around God. Now, don't mistake Isaiah's descriptions. These aren't little stubbly-faced winged dwarfs in diapers flying around with a bow and arrow of love. These are not little chubby babies with wings and harps flying around God's head like gnats.[2] On the contrary, we might be talking about mega-angels with lungs more powerful than jet engines.

During my junior year at Samford University in Birmingham, Alabama, LSU came to our little gym to practice for the Southeastern Conference basketball tournament. It was Shaquille O'Neal's senior year. I'll never forget Shaq standing under the basketball hoop as the team practiced free throws. Unbelievably, he placed his hand on the backboard, crossed his legs, and took a breather. Some people can't even jump and touch the backboard, and Shaq was standing flatfooted using it as a prop to take a load off. It was unbelievable. The truth is, the worshiping angels would make Shaq look like Gary Coleman.

Even more amazing is the thought that these angels are called "seraphs." The actual meaning for *seraph* is "burn." Thus, *seraphs* literally means "burning ones." Are you clueing in on what Isaiah is witnessing? He is seeing mega-angels flying and set afire by the burning holiness of God.

As if that isn't enough, these angels are covering their faces with two of their wings. So not only are these angels ablaze but God is burning so white-hot with holiness that they can't even look at him. With another two wings they cover their feet in awe and worship. And with two wings these massive burning angels flew around God. Can you imagine the sight? Can you even fathom what was going through Isaiah's brain?

These angels have never sinned. They have no idea what sin is. They have never been in the presence of sin. They are pure. But somehow—and it blows my gaskets to try to comprehend it—these angels in no way come close to the pure holiness of God. God's holiness has set them on fire! They cover their faces, unable to look upon this holy God, in the same way we cover our faces and shield our eyes from the sun.

On a plane a while back I had a conversation with a young businessman. I asked him what he believed it took to be saved and go to heaven. He believed that as long as we "made a good go of it," treated people well, and sacrificed a little for God, we'd be okay. "Really?" I asked. After further conversation, he admitted that he had lied before and once upon a time had had a dirty thought—in other words, he agreed that he had sinned before. I pointed him to Isaiah 6:2 and asked, "If these angels who were pure—had never sinned—were set ablaze in the holiness of God, covering their faces and feet, how could we possibly step into the presence of this holy God in heaven just by 'making a good go of it'? The Bible says that even our righteous acts are considered as 'filthy rags'" (Isa. 64:6; Prov. 30:12). He just sat and stared . . . then changed the subject.

Ringing Ears

And they were calling to one another: "Holy, holy, holy, is the LORD Almighty; the whole earth is full of his glory." At the sound of their

voices the doorposts and thresholds shook and the temple was filled
with smoke.

Isaiah 6:3–4

The angels' cries are cracking heavenly concrete and jarring
heaven's doors. The last time I checked, cupids and babies couldn't
do that.

My cousin Shannon once lived at the army base in Fort Sill,
Oklahoma. She told me about the jets and planes that would fly
over her home, rattling windows and walls. She also reminded me
of her experience going to Maxwell Air Force Base in Montgomery,
Alabama, to see the jet-flying team "The Thunderbirds." Now, talk
about power! We are talking about aircraft using 100,000 pounds
of jet thrust, flying at up to 1,200 miles per hour, and using only 60
percent power to go 3 miles straight up in the air.

At the show, the jets would perform a stunt where they would
fly directly above the crowd at the exact moment that they broke
the sound barrier. Shannon said when it happened, it shook everything: cars, poles, buildings, bodies. It was so loud that you felt the
concussion deep in your chest and your bones.

What did Isaiah hear? He heard burning angels with jet engine
lungs breaking the sound barrier: "HOLY [BOOM!], HOLY [BOOM!],
HOLY [BOOM!] is the LORD Almighty. . . ."

As all this was taking place, the temple began filling with smoke. I
remember seeing a magazine photo of the tragedy of September 11,
2001. A man was running for his life while glancing behind him at
a thick wall of smoke chasing him down the street. In the same way,
Isaiah is watching smoke snowball toward him, and like the man in
the photo, I bet he wants to run for his life.

This holy God is the God that the world does not know. He is
completely backward to the world. Ask a person on the street, "Who
is God to you?" and most would probably answer, "God is love."
Although this is true, there is more to God than love. The world
just wants to talk about the loving God: "A loving God wouldn't

do this. . . . A loving God wouldn't do that. . . ." But the fiery angels scream "holy, holy, holy," not "love, love, love." After *holy*, there are no words to explain the wonder of this awesome God. And to think, the angels didn't even stop at just "holy"—they cried, "holy, holy, holy!"

Gloriously Ruined

> "Woe to me!" I cried. "I am ruined! For I am a man of unclean lips, and I live among a people of unclean lips, and my eyes have seen the King, the LORD Almighty."
>
> Isaiah 6:5

This was the first time Isaiah could get anything to come out of his mouth. Did you catch his first word? Isaiah didn't say, "Cool!" or "Dude!" Isaiah cried, "Woe!" It was probably more like "Whooooooaaaa!" In today's language, Isaiah wailed the words, "I-AM-A-DEAD-MAN!"

In the week following the World Trade Center and Pentagon tragedies of September 11, 2001, I read an article in *USA Today* about the firemen who went into the Pentagon to look for survivors and to remove the dead. In the article, one of the firemen said that he walked through an office where there were two or three victims, each one still sitting in their original positions. There was a burned body still sitting in a chair with his hands up in front of his face as if he were reading something. Another charred body was still sitting at what was left of a desk in a posture showing that he had been writing something. Sadly yet mercifully, these people never knew what hit them. They were incinerated in an instant.

That is exactly what should have happened to Isaiah, and he knew it. He said it himself: "Woe to me! . . . I am ruined! I am a man of unclean lips, and I live among a people of unclean lips, and my eyes have seen the King, the LORD Almighty" (Isa. 6:5). He knew he was a sinner, and he knew that no sinner can come before the burning holiness of God and live, no matter how good a life he thinks he's lived. Why was Isaiah spared? Because God's full display of glory was hidden from him so that he would be spared. This was only a vision. God gave Isaiah just a glimpse—a glimpse that was still unbearable enough to make him think he would be destroyed. Isaiah was gloriously ruined.

Gloriously Rescued

> Then one of the seraphs flew to me with a live coal in his hand, which he had taken with tongs from the altar. With it he touched my mouth and said, "See, this has touched your lips; your guilt is taken away and your sin atoned for."
>
> Isaiah 6:6–7

It never fails: God is always the hero. Isaiah was a goner if God didn't do something. Yet God took it upon himself to make a way for Isaiah to be cleansed from his sin and saved from God's consuming holiness. Isaiah was in desperate need of rescue, and God made the way.

Let's detour a moment and make this truth clear. Has your soul registered why you and I are in such desperate need of a Savior? Do you see why being spiritual or religious, or going to church on Sunday, or having Christian parents, or serving at a homeless shelter on holidays, or "making a good go of it" doesn't save you? We are imprisoned by self and sin, and our God is "holy, holy, holy." If God doesn't make a way for us like he did for Isaiah, it's curtains for us.

Behold Jesus. God doesn't take a coal from an altar to cleanse our lips; he put his own Son on the altar of the cross to save our souls. Jesus took all of my sin and yours on the cross, and he's made the way for us to spend forever with this holy God—the One we are made for. Instead of fearing God's holiness, we now through faith dance in God's presence!

When we fully comprehend what took place on the cross, we will be awed by what God did to rescue us from ourselves—from our sin. At one time I was so mistaken about what happened to Jesus when he died on the cross. I believed that as God the Son (Jesus) hung there dying for our sin, God the Father was in heaven biting his fingernails, sobbing and distraught, with the angels barely able to hold him up. I pictured him peeking over heaven's edge, wailing, just wishing there was another way and yearning to do something, anything, to help Jesus but unable to do it. *Wrong!*

Let this portrait of what transpired on the cross between God the Son and God the Father awaken your soul.

> "Up you go!" They lift the cross. God is on display in his underwear and can scarcely breathe. But these pains are a mere warm-up to his coming suffering and growing dread. He begins to feel a foreign sensation. Sometime during this day an unearthly, foul odor begins to waft not around his nose but around his heart. He feels dirty. Human wickedness starts to crawl upon his spotless being—the living excrement from our souls. The apple of his Father's eye turns brown with rot.
>
> His Father! His Father! Must he face his Father like this?
>
> From heaven the Father now rouses himself like a lion disturbed, shakes his mane, and roars against the shriveling remnant of a man hanging on a cross. Never has the Son seen the Father look at him so, never felt even the least of his hot breath. But the roar shakes the unseen world and darkens the visible sky. The Son does not recognize these eyes.
>
> "Son of Man! Why have you behaved so? You have cheated, lusted, stolen, gossiped, murdered, envied, hated, lied. You have cursed, robbed, overspent, overeaten, fornicated, disobeyed, embezzled, blasphemed. Oh, the duties you have shirked, the children you have abandoned! Who has ever so ignored the poor, so played the coward, so belittled my name? Have you ever held your razor tongue? What a self-righteous pitiful drunk—you who molests young boys, peddles killer drugs, travels in cliques, and mocks your parents. Who gave you the boldness to rig elections, foment revolutions, torture animals, and

worship demons? Does the list ever end? Splitting families, raping virgins, acting smugly, playing the pimp, buying politicians, practicing extortion, filming pornography, accepting bribes. You have burned down buildings, perfected terrorist tactics, founded false religions, traded in slaves—relishing every morsel and bragging about it all. I hate, I loathe these things in you. Disgust for everything about you consumes me! Can you not feel my wrath?"

The Father watches as his heart's treasure, the mirror image of himself, sinks drowning into raw, liquid sin. Jehovah's rage, stored against humankind from every century, explodes in a single direction.

"Father! Father! Why have you forsaken me?"

But heaven stops its ears. The Son stares up at the One who cannot, who will not, reach down or reply. Two eternal hearts tear—their intimate friendship shaken to the depths.

The Trinity had planned it. The Son endured it. The Spirit enabled him. The Father rejected the Son whom he loved. Jesus, the God-man from Nazareth, perished. The Father accepted his sacrifice for sin and was satisfied. The rescue was accomplished.[3]

Jesus stepped into the ghetto of our world, took our sin upon himself, and his Father's holy wrath against that sin so that we might be rescued. We were goners but God made the way to save us through Jesus. Jesus endured the cross "for the joy set before him" (Heb. 12:2) because it would bring salvation to the souls of those who believe in him.

If anyone ever knew brokenness, it was Jesus. And for anyone to ever truly know Jesus, they must taste brokenness. Isaiah saw God in the temple and was nearly crushed. I saw God with my face buried in the carpet of my room and was gloriously ruined. It's just so backward. The world only preaches a God of puppy love who cuddles, yet God himself reveals that he is the holy One who ruins—gloriously ruins. Whose word will you take for it?

7

God Gone Public

> What if God was one of us?
>
> Joan Osborne,
> singer/songwriter

Inner-city Philadelphia—I was hangin' out at a community park and hoopin' it up with the locals. I was there off and on for about three weeks that summer.

Philly can get pretty hot in the summer. So every morning before heading to the park, some high school students who were there for mission projects and I would load up a cooler with bottled water, watermelon, apples, and so forth. Even when the high school students didn't go, I'd journey there by myself with at least a backpack full of bottled water and a couple of basketballs under my arms.

By the end of the first week the younger park kids were asking why I kept coming with water and watermelon for everybody. I suspected that some of the older guys had put them up to it. I can remember one kid in particular asking me and then running back to tell one of the rougher guys of the bunch what I said. He stared me down as he got the word. I always answered their questions with something like, "I just want you to know that Jesus Christ loves you. I just want to hang out if you'll let me and get to know you, play ball, and tell you a little more about Jesus and how he changed my life."

At first the locals weren't quite sure what to do with me. I was this tall guy from Alabama who talked funny and kept mentioning this "Jesus." But I could hold my own on the court. I wasn't cursing or picking fights or kicking things around when I missed a shot. Instead, I was encouraging people all the time. I was just, well, backward. I was an alien to them. I would like to think I was Christ's backward love to them.

The following week I went back with a new group of high school students. The younger kids on their bikes and skateboards started yelling: "It's holy man! It's holy man!" At the end of the second week, I was sitting on the cooler when a tough twelve-year-old kid walked up to me and said, "I love the devil." "Why?" I said. "Do you know what Jesus said about the devil? He wants to kill you, steal from you, and destroy everything you'll ever care about." With those statements I had a flock of about fifteen to twenty kids sitting, standing, and even lying down around me as I shared the gospel of Jesus. Although the older tough guys kept their distance, they were definitely curious.

Toward the end of the conversation, I asked what the kids thought. I asked if any of them wanted to have this Jesus as their Lord and Savior. Most of them just looked at each other, laughed, and started making fun of it all. But there were a few I could tell God had touched. Nobody became a Christian in that moment, but some left that day having heard the love, the truth, and the glory of the gospel of Jesus Christ.

After two weeks I had pegged the leader whom everyone looked up to. His name was Joe. We guarded each other on the court when we played against one another. We would chat here and there. I learned he was my age, had come from a rough upbringing, and was a bartender. I could tell everyone was a little scared of him. On a dime he would cuss you out, start a fight, and dog anyone he didn't like or who got on his nerves. Yet I felt that Joe respected me. He was a little abrupt and short with me when we talked, but he always shook my hand. Sometimes he asked me about my life, and he was at least cordial.

One day I was sitting with some of Joe's friends around a table and chatting. Joe walked up; he kept his distance but occasionally would throw in a comment or two as we all talked. Next thing I knew, everyone had gotten up to play another round of basketball. I took a gospel tract out of my bag and flipped it onto the table without anyone noticing. Joe was making his way by the table, saw the booklet, and picked it up, saying, "Whose is this?" With my heart racing and a lump in my throat, I stood up and said, "Oh, Joe, that's mine. It's about Jesus Christ, who . . ."

And before I could get the words out of my mouth Joe threw the tract back on the table, snatching his hands back from it like it was hot metal, saying, "Whooooaa."

As he turned to walk away, he cracked, "If God loves me, then he's going to have to come down here and show me!"

With everything in me, I wanted to run to Joe, grab him by the shoulders, and say, "Joe! God did come down here and show you. 'God showed his love among us: He sent his one and only Son into the world that we might live through him'" (1 John 4:9).

But it was not to be. I sissied out.

For weeks, months, Joe was heavy on my heart. I prayed for him. I even wept for him. Still today I wonder if Joe has encountered the God who through his Son went public by coming down here in skin, proving his love for Joe, for you, and for me. God went so far in his love for us that he died on a cross to save us. The proof of God's love and passion for Joe and for us is what this chapter is all about.

God Gone Public

The Creator became the creature. The Maker became the made. He who holds the earth's waters in the hollow of his hand and measures existence by the breadth of his hand came and walked among us. And his name was Jesus, the very "Word of God."

> In the beginning was the Word [Jesus], and the Word was with God, and the Word was God. He was with God in the beginning. Through him all things were made; without him nothing was made that has been made. In him was life, and that life was the light of men. The light shines in the darkness, but the darkness has not understood it.... The true light that gives light to every man was coming into the world. He was in the world, and though the world was made through him, the world did not recognize him. He came to that which was his own, but his own did not receive him. Yet to all who received him, to those who believed in his name, he gave the right to become children of God—children born not of natural descent, nor of human decision or a husband's will, but born of God. The Word became flesh and made his dwelling among us. We have seen his glory, the glory of the One and Only, who came from the Father, full of grace and truth.... No one has ever seen God, but God the One and Only, who is at the Father's side, has made him known.
>
> John 1:1–5, 9–14, 18

Can you grasp it? Jesus is the Creator God gone public. John 1:18 says, "No one has ever seen God, but God the One and Only, who is at the Father's side, has made him known." God "the One and Only" is Jesus. And Jesus made God the Father known, which really means he explained or demonstrated him. Jesus' ways, works, and words explained God. Jesus' life explains the mystery of the heart and love of God. How? Jesus, the very Word of God, is God!

> The Word was God.
>
> John 1:1

> The Word became flesh and made his dwelling among us.
>
> John 1:14

How backward can you get?

Some people have actually said that Jesus never said he was God. Yet in many places in the Gospels he claims he is. For the sake of space, time, and argument, I want you to see just one example that is often overlooked.

In the book of John chapter 8, Jesus is sparring with his own people—the Jews. They're insisting that they are "children of Abraham." Although this is true, Jesus argues that they are missing the greater spiritual reality. Basically Jesus tells them that if they were truly children of Abraham, they would believe he (Jesus) is God the Son—the "One and Only"—sent from God the Father. The Jews nearly lost their minds with this one. Jesus asks, "Can any of you prove me guilty of sin? If I am telling you the truth, why don't you believe me?" (John 8:46). Never a dirty thought, never a dirty word, no gossip, no cheating on taxes, no "little white lies," no *sin* ever came from Jesus. He was saying, "Hello, children of Abraham? Look at my life, look at my works, listen to my words! You mean you can't see it? I am the perfect one, the Messiah, the Word, the Son of God—God."

The Jews were fuming. So they tried to nail Jesus on his promise that if they believed in him, they would never see death (v. 51). "The Jews exclaimed, 'Now we know that you are demon-possessed! Abraham died and so did the prophets, yet you say that if anyone keeps your word, he will never taste death. Are you greater than our father Abraham? He died, and so did the prophets. Who do you think you are?'" (John 8:52–53).

After a few words about their stubborn unbelief, Jesus provoked the Jews even further with his comeback: "Your father Abraham rejoiced at the thought of seeing my day; he saw it and was glad" (v. 56).

Abraham's day was hundreds of years before Jesus. How could Jesus know that Abraham rejoiced at the thought of seeing his day come? How could he say, "I saw Abraham's face when he saw it all going down, and he was stoked"? So the Jews fired back: "'You are not yet fifty years old,' the Jews said to him, 'and you have seen Abraham!'" (v. 57).

Upon these words from the Jews, Jesus dropped a bombshell: "'I tell you the truth,' Jesus answered, 'before Abraham was born, I am!'" (v. 58).

In the Old Testament God appears to the prophet Moses through a burning bush. The message to Moses is that God would use him to lead the Israelites, God's people, out from the bondage and brutality of the Egyptians. Moses is extremely reluctant. So he asks God, "Suppose I go to the Israelites and say to them, 'The God of your fathers has sent me to you,' and they ask me, 'What is his name?' Then what shall I tell them?" Then God says to Moses, "This is what you are to say to the Israelites: 'I AM has sent me to you'" (Exod. 3:13–14).

Now take a glimpse back at the two little words Jesus uses at the end of his declaration to the Jews. "I tell you the truth," Jesus said, "before Abraham was born, *I AM!*" To the Jews, this declaration was absolute blasphemy. Jesus literally said, "I AM God."

Hold on to your beanies—Hebrews 1:8 is also staggering. It takes me to my knees in worship of Jesus. What am I talking about? See for yourself:

> But about the Son he says, "Your throne, O God, will last for ever and ever."
>
> Hebrews 1:8

Did you catch it? It's the Father calling the Son . . . *God*! In other words, God the Father turns and says to the Son (Jesus), "God, your throne will last for ever and ever." Jesus is God gone public.

God Became Flesh to Pursue You

It's true. God became one of us. The holy God, through his Son, took on skin and moved to the ghetto of planet earth. It was the only way for us to be saved. This is why Jesus is the only way to heaven. He's God in the flesh.

If you've ever doubted, let me tell you, God is passionate for you. He put on skin and came after you. And even right now he's pursued you through this very book, all the way to this very moment. Are you dying inside? He's the giver of life. Do you wonder if anyone notices you? He's constantly whispering your name. Do you feel so misunderstood that you are on the brink of giving up? He understands you intimately. He knows your thoughts before you think them, your words before you speak them.

I once owned a guinea pig. I loved that little thing. But it was hard to love him because he was so scared of me. I did all I could to try to show the little guinea piggie how much I loved him and that he didn't have to be afraid of me. I placed a little salt lick in his cage. I dropped in a toy or two. I slipped in lettuce and carrots every now and then. Every day I'd bend down and lean in toward the cage and speak the love language of guinea "piganese" to him. No matter what I did, every time my shadow darkened his cage, he would back himself into a corner, curl into a knot, tremble all over, and squeal until he lost his voice. Even though I loved him, I couldn't make him understand.

Then a spiritual truth hit me: the only way I could make the guinea pig know how much I loved him would be to become a guinea pig myself and enter into the cage of his world. Talk about a backward life! But think about it. Giving up my humanity and becoming like a guinea pig—fat, furry, ratlike, eating grain pellets, drinking stagnant water, snacking on gooey brown lettuce, sleeping on poopy-soaked wood chips, and running on a little wheel that goes nowhere—would show that I love him. But would I really give up my life to move into the fur and cage of a guinea pig? Give me a break. . . .

Isn't that what God did, though? God went public through his Son Jesus Christ, stepping out of the glorious heavenly realm where he was worshiped by trillions of angels twenty-four hours a day, seven days a week. He entered a dark womb and was born into our broken human world with one mission: to die for us. He entered into our cage. He, the backward God, took on our pain, our darkness, our fears, our burdens. He didn't become a guinea pig because we're not guinea pigs. We're flesh, so he became flesh and lived among us (see John 1:14).

Take Me Instead

Sin placed a gulf wider than all the light years you can dream of between us and the holy God. Apart from God and left in our sin, we were dead, because sin absolutely destroys lives and souls. So before the foundation of the world, God put in motion a time when he would become flesh, dwell among us without sin, and go to the cross in our place as the perfect sacrifice for our sin so that we might live. On the cross Jesus took on your sin and mine and paid the death penalty for us.

> God made him who had no sin to be sin for us, so that we might become the righteousness of God.
>
> 2 Corinthians 5:21

Years ago I read a story about a kid named Stephen that parallels a great spiritual truth. In the 1990s Stephen and his mom took a horseback-riding trip in the mountains of Canada. As they were riding along, a cougar came out of nowhere and attacked Stephen. Stephen's mom did what any mom would have done. She got off of her horse and started jumping up and down, screaming and waving her arms, trying to draw the cat's attention off her son onto her. It worked. The cougar left Stephen and attacked his mom. Stephen managed to crawl for help. By the time he returned, it was too late. Stephen's mother was killed by the vicious cat. She gave her life so that Stephen might live.

Like a deadly predator, sin was viciously attacking, biting, clawing, and destroying our lives and souls. Jesus spread out his arms on the cross and cried out, "Take me instead!" What does that mean? It means Jesus took on the sin and death that was meant for you and me, with all its destruction and hell, so that through faith in him, you and I might live the life we're meant for—abundant life—now and forevermore.

The Blood of God

Let's put things in perspective.

When my mom and dad were dating, they would hang out at the local Dairy Queen in my hometown of Clanton, Alabama. One night some extremely mean teenagers caught a stray dog, poured gas all over it, and set it on fire. The dog yelped and yelped and ran under a car, where it slowly burned to death. My mom and dad were horrified beyond belief.

Now, let me ask you something. As you read that, what was your reaction? I bet your mouth was open. I bet your heart sank into your guts. You may have felt rage. You may have teared up a bit. You may even be upset with me for sharing such a story. But here's the crux of the matter. We get more upset over the cruelty committed to a stray dog (now, granted, there's reason to be very upset by this) than we do over the cruelty Jesus suffered. People like you and me are responsible for murdering the Son of God, the God-man, sinless, perfect, innocent Jesus, on a cross. Nonetheless, though humanity is responsible for Jesus' death, Jesus would not have died unless he himself chose to go to the cross for us.

> And being found in appearance as a man, he humbled himself and became obedient to death—even death on a cross!
>
> Philippians 2:8

How do you explain this passion that would cause the perfect Son of God to choose to die for you and me? One word keeps coming to mind: backward. If there's anyone who did not deserve to be tortured and killed like a thief and murderer, it was Jesus. You know what I'm saying? That wasn't Adolf Hitler on a cross. That was *God* on a cross . . . dying for you and dying for me. Think of Jesus' blood trickling down the wood. That blood is the blood of God.

In reality it should have been you and me up there—our sin devouring us, God's wrath consuming us. But Jesus took our place. On the cross it's your sin he's feeling, your death he's dying, and your life and soul he's saving—if you believe.

A Gruesome Beauty

The cross is a gruesome thing. But looking backward, it's beautiful. When Jesus died on the cross, he took our sin with him. But if it ended at Jesus' death, we'd still be in trouble—in trouble because sin and death would have beaten him. But three days later there was a grave with no Jesus. Jesus was alive, proving that he is who he said he was (more on the resurrection later). Jesus is God gone public. And there is no way to get to God, except through God—Jesus Christ.

Life—purpose, fulfillment, satisfaction, peace, hope, joy, freedom—was released through Jesus' life, sacrifice, and resurrection (John 10:10). This life, the backward life, is not something we reach for. It is within us.

> You will make known to me the path of life; in Your presence is the fullness of joy. In Your right hand are pleasures forever.
>
> Psalm 16:11 NASB

Jesus is the path of true life and eternal life. As C. S. Lewis said, we are far too easily pleased in settling for life, happiness, and sin in things of the world instead of pursuing the ultimate pleasure of our souls—Jesus. In Jesus we discover the answers of life and eternity. In Jesus we are freed to discover the God we were made for and the life we are meant for—the backward life.

The Shout of God

This God of glory is coming back. Jesus himself said that one day people will see him "coming in a cloud with power and great glory" (Luke 21:27). Next time there will be no cave, no feeding trough, no cross, no death. Jesus will come down from the heavens in raw power and roaring glory to take his people home.

> Listen, and I will tell you a secret. We shall not all die, but suddenly, in the twinkling of an eye, every one of us will be changed as the trumpet sounds! For the trumpet will sound and the dead shall be raised beyond the reach of corruption, and we who are still alive shall suddenly be utterly changed.
>
> 1 Corinthians 15:51–52 Phillips

> For the Lord Himself will descend from heaven with a shout, with the voice of the archangel, and with the trumpet of God; and the dead in Christ shall rise first. Then we who are alive and remain will be caught up together with them in the clouds to meet the Lord in the air, and so we shall always be with the Lord.
>
> 1 Thessalonians 4:16–17 NASB

On a Sunday in December of 1999, I was speaking at a small church in Enterprise, Alabama. I overheard people talking about something that had happened earlier in the morning. At around 4:00 a.m., they and many others heard a loud "KABOOM!" It was so loud that it rattled their windows and jolted them out of the bed. They shook their heads talking about how it had scared them to death. One of them thought a gas station had exploded.

I later learned that the same sound had been heard over different parts of the South. All day I wondered what in the world it was. Later that night news broadcasts revealed that a small meteor had hit the earth's atmosphere, causing the thunderous, bomblike explosion that made southern folk leap straight up out of their beds in shock.

Here's the deal: If you think a little meteor hitting the earth's atmosphere was loud, wait until Jesus "hits" the atmosphere ... with a shout! Jesus is going to give a shout that's not going to be heard by just a few southerners—it's going to be heard by the whole universe. And it's going to do a lot more than rattle windows and wake up church folk. It's going to rattle the universe and wake the dead ... and end the world as we know it.

> He [Jesus] who testifies to these things says, "Yes, I am coming soon." Amen. Come, Lord Jesus.
>
> Revelation 22:20

Where Are You, Joe?

Even though it's been years since I've been to inner-city Philly, I still think about Joe. I wonder what he's doing; I wonder if he's okay; I wonder if he's in prison or even still alive. I wonder if Joe became a believer, which would mean that one day I will meet him again "up there" or "in the air."

I wish I could go back to that moment when Joe said that God would have to show up and prove his love for Joe. I wish I could go back and by God's grace have the courage to stop him in his tracks and say, "Joe, he did. God became flesh to pursue you; he became sin to rescue you; he embraced death to save you; he released life to free you; and he's coming again for you, Joe."

What do you think? Are you like Joe, needing God to prove to you that he loves you? Think of the feeding trough in which the infant God was laid. Gaze at the cross upon which the Savior God was hung. Look up at the clouds from which the Lord God will come to take you home. What more proof do you need?

8

Just Because

REDUCE THE ENGLISH LANGUAGE TO JUST 3 SYLLABLES:
I. LOVE. YOU.
DIAMONDS ARE FOREVER.

advertisement in a walkway of an international airport

"A re They for Real?" reads the headline of an article in the *Houston Chronicle* about celebrity "love" a few years ago.[1] The article was questioning whether celebrity couples were truly in love. Included were photos of couples like Jessica Simpson and Nick Lachey, and Tom Cruise and Penelope Cruz (all of whom have since split).

The main focus of the article was not the love of these celebrities but the then-recent split between Ben Affleck and Jennifer Lopez, better known as "Ben and J-Lo" or "Bennifer." Ben and Jennifer have since moved on, of course. But there's still something about this I want you to ponder. In the newspaper, with a picture of J-Lo's engagement ring, the front-page headlines read, "Should J-Lo Keep

It?" That was a great question since the ring was worth 1.2 million stinkin' dollars!

The celebrity scene mirrors, or perhaps shapes, what we think love should be. We express our love by giving stuff, a lot of stuff, expensive stuff, to those we intimately love. Is that really what love is about? Is giving stuff an expression of guaranteed, authentic, to-the-death love? Are diamond rings, even a 1.2 million dollar diamond ring, proof of a love that is forever? Ask Ben and J-Lo now.

What if God loved like that? I mean, what if God loved us so much that he expressed it in just that way, by giving us a lot of stuff? Some of us might think that's not too bad a deal. We like stuff—diamond rings, flowers, Xbox 360s, Harley Davidsons, Ferraris, golf clubs, two-story houses, surround-sound stereo systems. But a husband can "love" his wife with flowers, chocolates, and diamonds while sleeping around with another woman; it happens all the time. And believe me, that kind of love is the polar opposite of the love of Jesus. What if God "loved" by giving us everything we've ever wanted—Hummers, toned bodies, fame—yet condemned us to a life in hell without him forever? While human love is masked by stuff, God reveals a love that reaches the outer limits of our comprehension and keeps on trucking:

> For God so loved the world that he gave his one and only Son, that whoever believes in him shall not perish but have eternal life.
>
> John 3:16

The danger here is that I can lose you right now. Most Americans and others around the world recognize this piece of Bible real estate. Remember the guy in the crowd at WWF matches and pro football games waving the John 3:16 poster? The first time you ever talked about religion and Christianity, John 3:16 popped up, I'm sure. If you grew up in church, John 3:16 and "Jesus wept" (John 11:35) were the first two Scripture verses you memorized. So by clueing in on where I'm now going in this chapter, you might actually be clueing out.

Have you ever watched a movie or read a book for a second, third, or fifteenth time and noticed things you didn't notice before? Ever read a letter or email (perhaps a love letter) again and again and found wonderful, moving messages you missed the first few times around? Well, let's go to the spiritual attic and blow the dust off John 3:16 again. It may be a trip down memory lane for many of you. But don't take anything for granted. Threaded through each word is a love so unimaginable, it's backward.

For God

It all begins with God. God is always the subject of the sentence, not us. God is always the hero. He is holy, holy, holy. Remember the colossal, sinless angels set afire by God's holiness, shielding their faces, covering their feet? With jet engine lungs and voices that break the sound barrier, they cry out, "Holy, holy, holy, is the LORD Almighty; the whole earth is full of his glory" (Isa. 6:3). Remember Isaiah's response? "Whoooaa . . . I'm a dead man!" God is not just the God who loves but the God who gloriously ruins us by his holiness.

After hearing over and over again that God is love, love, love, is it any wonder that he seems uninteresting? Is it any wonder that yawns of indifference surface before God instead of shouts of praise to God? But the God of heaven and earth is anything but uninteresting. If yawning and boredom set in like a hangover when you think of God, perhaps you're seeing only the "bright side" of God, his love. That's like trying to enjoy fireworks on the sunny sands of a Florida beach at noon. To know the splendor of the love of God, to behold the beauty and power of the fireworks of his love, it must be seen against the backdrop of the midnight sky of his holy wrath.[2]

If God was holy, holy, holy alone, it would be curtains for us. Think of it this way: If all God told us was that he was holy and wrathful against sin, we would run in fear for our lives, knowing we were condemned to die. We would never want him. Guilt would overwhelm us. We'd walk around with clenched eyes, expecting God to kill us at any second. But John 3:16 doesn't stop with "For God . . ."

So Loved

Woo-hoo! Starting to feel like you should be shouting instead of yawning? This white-hot burning holy God *loves*. No, he doesn't just love, he *so* loves! Look at it again: "For God so loved." "So" implies great intensity. The Phillips translation of John 3:16 says it this way: "For God loved the world so much. . . ."

Christie and I are on the go constantly. Josiah practically lives in a car seat. Josiah is much clingier with Christie than he is with me. Pulling into the driveway one night, I asked Christie if I could get Josiah out of the car seat and put him to bed while she got the stroller and baby bag. I carefully undid the straps, picked him up, and laid him on my chest. He wrapped his arms around me and buried his face into my neck. I could feel his little heartbeat. I could feel his hot breath as he snuggled into me. I walked into his room and just stood there holding him. I didn't want to put him down. Christie stuck her head in and encouraged me to put him down before he woke up (or I'd be the one up with him all night). I said, "Okay, just give me a minute. I don't want to miss this moment. He'll be a teenager tomorrow." Then I laid him down, put my hand on his chest, prayed over him, kissed him on the forehead, and whispered, "I love you so much, my son Josiah."

With tears in my eyes I walked back toward our bedroom, pulling off my shirt and getting ready for bed. As I walked into the room with the shirt dangling from my hand, God whispered, "Jarrod, you think that's love? Son, this is love. . . ."

> This is love: not that we loved God, but that he loved us and sent his Son as an atoning sacrifice for our sins.
>
> 1 John 4:10

God's backward love: God loved, so loved, when we didn't love him. It's easy to love my wife, my family, and my friends because they love me back. It's not so easy to love people when they don't love me. And it's all but impossible to love those who cheat us, use us, reject us, abandon us, and forget about us. Awhile back, J-Lo may have said, "This is love" as Ben put the 1.2 million dollar ring on her finger, but God said, "No, this is love" and gave his Son to die for us—we who didn't love him. When I put the puny little engagement ring on Christie's finger, no doubt she thought, "Wow, this ring shows me Jarrod loves me." But God, in his love for us, shows his love in a way that is beyond words—he gave himself in the form of his Son to suffer and die for a world that hated him. It makes no human sense. It's just plain backward.

> This is how God showed his love among us: He sent his one and only Son into the world that we might live through him.
>
> 1 John 4:9

For God So Loved . . . the World

God so loved the world. Why? I don't understand it. I can't get my fingers around it. God so loves a world that hates him. You and I have yelled "I'm number one!" with the American number one sign, the spiritual bird finger, in God's face.

> There is no one righteous, not even one;
>> there is no one who understands,
>> no one who seeks God.
> All have turned away,
>> they have together become worthless;
> there is no one who does good,
>> not even one.
> Their throats are open graves;
>> their tongues practice deceit.

The poison of vipers is on their lips.
Their mouths are full of cursing and
    bitterness.
Their feet are swift to shed blood;
    ruin and misery mark their ways,
and the way of peace they do not
    know.
There is no fear of God before their
    eyes.

                         Romans 3:10–18

Ravi Zacharias shares a story about a young woman whose husband had gone to a prayer meeting on a Wednesday night. Late that evening the young woman went to take some clothes off a clothesline when a man came through the bushes and forced her inside with his gun. She had just given birth to a baby weeks before. The baby was her third child. While her other children were locked in their rooms, the intruder took the baby in his arms, put the barrel of the gun to the baby's temple, and warned the young woman that if she didn't do what he said he would blow the baby's brains apart. The woman quickly did as she was told, and according to Zacharias, he "mercilessly raped her."

Seven months later Zacharias had opportunity to sit down and counsel this young woman. She wept uncontrollably. She wept intensely about her problems with the relationship with her husband, society, and God. He asked if she could just explode out in a burst of emotion in one statement of her heartfelt feelings and pain, and she cried out, "I'VE BEEN VIOLATED!"[3]

Our sin violates God's holiness. Now, it didn't take him by surprise nor force itself upon him. On the contrary, God saw it coming and had every right to unleash his holy wrath to literally incinerate the world like a plastic straw in a raging bonfire. So again it raises the question, why didn't God crush the world? Why didn't God just hit the delete button on a world that flipped him off?

Adam and Eve ate the "off-limits" fruit; Noah got drunk; Moses killed a man; Israel grumbled, complained, and rebelled constantly; King David, a man after God's own heart, committed adultery and murder; and we cheat, lie, and worship "me, me, me." Any minute it seems God might roar: "You people! You will never get it! I am *done* with you!" *Delete.*

I bet that's what the shepherds thought. There they were in the fields one night, watching their sheep. All of a sudden an angel cracked the sky. Onto their backs they fell, terrified, and with trembling voices they probably screamed, "We're dead! This is it. It's over." But the angel said, "Shhhhhh. Don't be afraid. Today I've got good news for you and the whole world! In the town a Savior has been born to you, and he is Christ the Lord" (see Luke 2:8–12).

Why did God do it? Well, just because.... Just because God so loved the world.

You see, while God is holy, holy, holy, he is also love. But understand this: He does not have a split personality as some might suggest. He is not sometimes holy and at other times love. He is not an Old Testament God on Mondays and a New Testament God on weekends. He is constantly holy, holy, holy, and love, love, love at the same time. He's consistent, never changing, the same forever and ever.

For God so loved the world . . .

That He Gave

I don't have to spend a lot of time here, do I? It's pretty clear. We can't earn anything from God. He's too holy; he's too great; he's too giving; he's too loving. We can't even hold a candle to his sunlike glory. So what he gives—laughter, children, chocolate ice cream, friendships—are all gifts. Through his greatest gift, Jesus, we are given the gift of life's joys that we take for granted every day.

You can't stack enough "good works" to the stars to earn your place in heaven. You could work at the homeless shelter every Thanksgiving holiday for the rest of your life, and you'd still be stuck in the mud of "self" and sin. Even as much as Mother Teresa sacrificed by giving her life to the poorest of the poor and the sickest of the sick, she got about as close to earning God's love as Fargo, North Dakota, is to Pluto.

John 3:16 doesn't say that we loved and gave God so much that we earned his one and only Son. Rather, God loved us so much that he *gave* us his Son. Salvation is a gift. You can't earn it. You can't merit it. You can't warrant it. It's all God, and it's all a gift.

> For it is by grace that you have been saved, through faith—and this not from yourselves, it is the gift of God—not by works, so that no one can boast.
>
> Ephesians 2:8–9

He Gave His One and Only Son

For God so loved the world that he gave diamonds? Sent roses? No. For God so loved the world that he gave himself, in the form of his one and only Son.

Let me reiterate what I said in a previous chapter, because it's important: Jesus never sinned. Jesus never thought an evil thought, never lusted for a woman, never lied about his age, and never gossiped about the lady on the street corner. Some people don't believe this. A couple of years ago I was in West Virginia, where I met a man standing at the fence around his yard. After talking with him about the weather and sports, I asked him what he thought about Jesus. He said he appreciated the fact that Jesus was just like us and had "made mistakes" (sinned) before. My new friend was both right and wrong. Yes, Jesus was just like us. He got tired, he got onion breath, he got headaches, he stubbed his toe, and he was tempted by Satan. But he never, ever, not even one time, sinned. As Hebrews 4:15 says,

> For we do not have a high priest who is unable to sympathize with our weaknesses, but we have one who has been tempted in every way, just as we are—yet was without sin.

That's what makes the cross so terrible. Jesus—innocent, perfect, sinless, God—on a cross dying for a world who hated him. And what makes it even more amazing is that people like you and me crucified Jesus on a cross, but he went there because he wanted to. Truth be told, the Jews and Romans didn't kill Jesus. God killed Jesus.

> We all, like sheep, have gone astray, each of us has turned to his own way; and the LORD has laid on him the iniquity of us all. . . . Yet it was the LORD's will to crush him and cause him to suffer.
>
> Isaiah 53:6, 10

Jesus stepped out of the glory of heaven and into the ghetto of the world and took on the sin of the world. With the sin of the world upon him, Jesus hung on a cross as the perfect sacrifice, satisfying the wrath of the holy God. He was crushed by God's wrath against sin, and he died in our place. This is not divine child abuse. As mentioned earlier, Jesus went to the cross "for the joy set before him" (Heb. 12:2). Jesus willingly went to the cross, to be crushed by God's holiness, in place of you and me. Now that's love . . . a backward love.

Remember, God is both holy and love. He loves you, yes. But because he is holy, holy, holy and because you are a sinner, sinner, sinner, in his holy presence you will die.

On August 16, 1987, Northwest flight 255 departed Detroit headed to Phoenix. A failure to adjust wing flaps following takeoff caused the pilots to lose control of the plane. The plane plummeted toward the earth, crashing on Interstate 94. Many on the ground were killed. Everyone aboard the plane died except one little girl,

Cecilia Cichan. The experts were baffled. How in the world did she survive? They discovered that as the plane was falling out of the sky, Cecilia's mother unlatched her safety belt, somehow crawled over on top of Cecilia, and wrapped her body around her child, shielding her from the destruction of the fire, the debris, and the wrath of that plane crash. Cecilia lived.[4]

What happened on the cross? Jesus wrapped his life around you, taking on the destruction of the wrath of a holy God, so that you might live. "This is love: not that we loved God, but that he loved us and sent his Son as an atoning sacrifice for our sins" (1 John 4:10).

For God so loved the world that he gave his one and only Son . . .

Whoever Believes in Him

Do you hold on to colossal guilt and shame over the mistakes you've made in your life? I know people who have made the "mistake" of adultery, brought about the "mistake" of abortion in someone's life, or made the "mistake" of wrecking their body with sex, smoke, drink, or drugs. You may be like them: staring at the crossroads for years, unable to cross over to embrace the God of total freedom. You think you must be punished somehow, some way. So you wait. You wait for the tragedy, the sickness, the abandonment, the sorrow that you think you deserve and that are sure to come because of what you did in your past.

We all have a pile of "mistakes." Nowhere does God say, "If you only have one mistake, then I'll talk to you when you complete six weeks of good behavior. If you have two mistakes, don't come near me until you've gone to church for a year. If you have three mistakes, I'll never talk to you again. If you have five mistakes, you're dead."

Forget that! (I know, that's easy to say, hard to do.) One of God's favorite words is "come." Jesus said, "Come to me, all you who are weary and burdened, and I will give you rest" (Matt. 11:28). It's a bit cliché now, but it fits so well: You don't clean up your life and then come to Jesus. You come to Jesus and then he will clean up your life.

Please listen. You don't have to be punished for your past before you come to Jesus. Jesus already took your punishment—on the cross. That's why he said, "whoever." With a smile on his face, love in his heart, and compassion in his voice, Jesus says, "Whoever has committed adultery, whoever has had abortions, whoever is an alcoholic . . . come."

> For God so loved the world that he gave his one and only Son, that whoever . . .

Does that mean Jesus saves everyone? No. Jesus only saves people who come to him by believing in him and him alone. Jesus saves those who confess that God is holy, holy, holy and that they are sinners who cannot save themselves. Jesus saves those who turn from "self" (sin) and trust that he is the Son of God—the God-man who came to earth, lived without sin, died on a cross for our individual sins, and rose on the third day. The God who is now seated at the right hand of God the Father in heaven and will return to earth one day in all his glory to take his children home.

Believing is not agreeing. Here lies the danger. You can read everything I just said and agree with it: "Yeah, okay, Jesus was the Son of God, he died on a cross, he rose from the dead, yada, yada, yada, I got it." That's not belief.

There are two types of belief—one that agrees, and one that saves. You can "believe" in Jesus the same way you believe that George Washington was the first president of the United States. This is how demons believe. James 2:19 says, "You believe that there is one God. Good! Even the demons believe that—and shudder." This "belief" of the demons doesn't save them.

So what does it mean to believe? When I was in college, some friends and I would go to Oak Mountain State Park in Birmingham, Alabama, on some Sunday afternoons to just get away, throw a Frisbee, and hang out. One particular Sunday, I was standing on the shore of Oak Mountain Lake, about toe deep, and was throwing the Frisbee with a few of the guys. As I was waiting for my turn, I turned around and noticed this little boy about twenty feet behind me playing in the water. He caught my attention because he was a tiny fellow playing all by himself, with no mother or father or anyone else in sight.

After throwing the Frisbee for a few more minutes, I turned around and saw the kid was gone. I looked around everywhere but didn't see him. I couldn't believe he had gotten past me without me even noticing it. But as I turned to catch the Frisbee again, something in the water caught my eye. A little hand came out from under the water and went back under again.

The lake at Oak Mountain State Park is man-made. Beginning at the shoreline of the lake is a concrete slab that runs under the water about 30 feet out into the water. The slab runs at a downward slope and then abruptly stops. So I could be 29 feet out, and the water would be up to my thighs. But if I took another step, I'd step off of the concrete slab, and the water would be up to my chest. This little boy had stumbled off the concrete slab, and he was drowning. My first reaction was to dive. So I dove, all six-foot-seven and 240 pounds of me, into about 18 inches of water. It was just one big "thud." My teammates, even the whole beach, thought I had just freaked out for no reason. I had to scrape myself up off the concrete, with dirt and grime all in my hair and eyes, cuts and scratches on my nose and chest, and do that bow-legged, high-step run through the water to get to the little boy.

When I got to him he was staring straight up through the water with eyes as big as saucers, and he was not moving. I reached down into the water, snatched him up, held him tight against my chest, and patted him on his back, saying, "I got you, little man, I got you." The little boy went from crying to squirming, then to wrapping his little arms around me, hanging on to me for dear life. He knew if it wasn't for me he was a goner. He clung to me like Velcro.

That's belief. It's banking your life on the truth that without the cross of Jesus, you are a goner. It's pinning your hopes and dreams on the reality that without Jesus pulling you out of your sin, you will spiritually drown and die. It's clinging to Jesus, wrapping your spiritual arms and legs around him, digging your nails into his back with all your heart and with all your might, as if your life and soul depended on it—because they do. It's holding fast to him like a drowning child. That is belief.

> For God so loved the world that he gave his one and only Son, that whoever believes in him . . .

Shall Not Perish

It ought to be clear now that without Jesus, we perish. But perish how? Perish where?

You can perish in this life. I don't mean perish in the sense that you'll get cancer, you'll never get married, you'll wind up in a wheelchair, your husband will leave you, your house will burn down, or you'll go bankrupt (although many Christ-followers have these experiences too). I mean perish in the sense that your life will be vain and futile and you will have no lasting, deep-down peace, joy, fulfillment, or purpose. You'll never know what you are made for. You'll waste your life clambering around and chasing mirages of happiness through how-to best sellers, the latest dieting trends, and lover after lover. Life, the life you were meant for, will escape you. You'll be like my parents' dog that chased the light from the flashlight that I had pointed toward the floor. Scrambling, chasing, barking, biting, but never getting what you're after, never tasting anything but a mouthful of linoleum.

That's not the worst of it. Not only will you perish in this life, but even more horrifying, you will perish in the next life. These words are truth. You will live forever . . . somewhere. The Bible makes it clear that the choices of ultimate destiny are heaven or hell. Jesus talked a whole lot about hell, even more than he did heaven. Without the Savior Jesus, your destiny (and mine) is hell. Hell, according to Jesus, is a place of eternal torture, the blackest darkness, the lake of sulfurous fire, weeping, gnashing of teeth, and a place where the worm never dies. It's a place meant for Lucifer and his cronies after they rebelled against God. It's also a place for those who rebel against God by not embracing his Son as their Savior. Just check this out:

> [They] will drink of the wine of God's fury, which has been poured full strength into the cup of his wrath. [They] will be tormented with burning sulfur in the presence of the holy angels and of the Lamb. And the smoke of their torment rises for ever and ever. There is no rest day or night.
>
> Revelation 14:10–11

Sounds like hell, doesn't it? Well, it is. Hell is the full destructive power of God's wrath poured out forever and ever on those who refuse Jesus. Through God's Son Jesus, right now God offers mercy, forgiveness, and salvation to people who have violated him by their sin (that would be all of us). Hell is God's last resort. Choose not to accept God's offer, and all mercy is gone and God's wrath is poured out like Niagara Falls forever and ever on all who have refused Jesus and trusted in self, religion, or anything else to save them.

Look back at Revelation 14:10–11. Did you notice whose presence is mentioned? The holy angels and the Lamb, Jesus. At its core, hell is God minus grace, God minus mercy, God minus love . . . forever.

There will be worship in hell. Philippians 2:9–11 says,

> Therefore God exalted him to the highest place and gave him the name that is above every name, that at the name of Jesus every knee should bow, in heaven and on earth and under the earth, and every

tongue confess that Jesus Christ is Lord, to the glory of God the
Father.

Knees will bow in hell before Jesus; tongues will confess in hell
to Jesus that he is Lord of all. Jesus will be there for it all. In hell,
God will be present in his explosive wrath, and people who have
rejected God all of their lives and not embraced Jesus as their personal Savior will be consumed by darkness, pain, and regret that
defies imagination, forever. There is only one hope for those who
long for the destiny they were meant for: Jesus.

For God so loved the world that he gave his one and only Son, that
whoever believes in him shall not perish . . .

But Have Eternal Life

Eternal life is not just length of life but quality of life. You can
get a taste of eternal life in the here and now, on earth. "I have come
that they may have life, and have it to the full," Jesus said (John
10:10). Not a half-full or half-empty glass of life, not a mediocre
experience of life, not a "get through the week" life, not a "paycheck to paycheck" life, not an "eke out an existence" life, but a *full*
life—that's the life you were meant for. As Matt Chandler (lead
pastor at the Village Church, Highland Village, Texas) once said,
Jesus makes the good times better, the mediocre times purposeful,
and the horrific times glorious. In other words, Jesus gives a life
filled with purpose, freedom, joy, and contentment no matter what
your personal circumstances, no matter what people say or do to
you. It's like the bumper sticker says: NO JESUS, NO PEACE. KNOW
JESUS, KNOW PEACE.

What about the next life? What is the ultimate destiny for those
who believe in Jesus? Scripture says, "No eye has seen, no ear has
heard, no mind has conceived what God has prepared for those who
love him" (1 Cor. 2:9).

We can try to imagine the glories of heaven all day long but never come close. Not to worry. If you *believe*, God gives you the gift of his Holy Spirit, who lifts you up to what awaits you:

> Now the dwelling of God is with men, and he will live with them. They will be his people, and God himself will be with them and be their God. He will wipe every tear from their eyes. There will be no more death or mourning or crying or pain, for the old order of things has passed away.
>
> Revelation 21:3–4

You will have an existence without pain, tears, cancer, and funerals. A life overwhelmed with the love of a God who made you and whom you were made for . . . forever and ever.

Did you catch who's going to be Daddy in heaven? Did you notice who's going to cup your face in his hands and wipe away your tears? It won't be the pope, it won't be a pastor, and it won't be an angel. The holy God himself will wipe away every tear from your eyes.

> For God so loved the world that he gave his one and only Son, that whoever believes in him shall not perish but have eternal life!

It's Just Backward

God loves us. He won't give us everything we've ever wanted, but he will give us everything we've hoped for. He loves us so much that he doesn't give us all the diamonds, roses, and chocolates of the world. He loves us infinitely more. It's backward to our human desires. He loves us so much more that he gave himself, in the form of his Son, to die so that we might live with him forever.

For crying out loud, how amazing is this love of God? We will never grasp it in this life. I feel like the little boy who crawled into the lap of his father and asked, "Dad, why is the sky blue? Why is the grass green? Why don't cats bark and dogs meow? Why do you love me?" "Well, son," the father answers, "just because."

How about you? Go ahead. Crawl into his lap. Ask him, "Daddy, why do you love me?" Then feel the heartbeat of God for you as he gently whispers in your ear, "My child, I love you. I love you . . . just because."

That's Incredible

There goes my hero.

The Foo Fighters,
"My Hero"

After high school I attended Brewer State (now Bevill State) Junior College in Fayette, Alabama. While I was there a rumor was going around about the college's professor of chemistry. We called him "Doc." The rumor was that he could place his hands in a container of sulfuric acid—acid that will disintegrate a metal spoon in a matter of seconds—wash his hands in it, pat it on his face, and walk away without even so much as chapped skin. I didn't believe it for a second. But my friends tried to convince me it was true. They told me he even had a videotape of his sulfuric acid bath from when he had appeared on a popular '80s television show called *That's Incredible!*

I finally worked up the courage to ask Doc about it. He said it was true. He invited a friend and me over that night to see the video for ourselves. There was no way on the planet I was going to pass this up. In the video he was standing on stage with the host, Fran

Tarkanten, and in front of him was a clear container of sulfuric acid. To my recollection, Doc took a spoon and placed it into the acid, and the spoon melted away. Amazingly, he then placed his hands into the same acid and rubbed it onto his face. The camera zoomed in on Fran Tarkanten's face. He stared into the camera and spouted off the show's famous words: "That's incredible!"

I confess, after all of the evidence—from the claims of Doc's former students, to his testimony, to the videotape—I walked out of his apartment that night a believer.

In the Gospel of John, a man named Thomas felt perhaps the same way you do. He was a close follower of Jesus, a disciple for nearly three years. After seeing Jesus die on the cross, he had a hard time believing that there was any way Jesus could be alive, raised from the dead. It was just too incredible. Even today many who call themselves "Christians" believe most of what Jesus said and did but not that Jesus was the Son of God who rose from the dead. They are "doubting Thomases." But God doesn't give up on these doubters, just as he didn't give up on Thomas. And he hasn't given up on you.

Where's Thomas?

It's a Sunday, the third day after Jesus' crucifixion, and the disciples are all crowded into somebody's apartment with the doors bolted and locked. They're probably finishing off the leftover roast beef and potato salad from the funeral memorial. Jesus shows up on the scene. No doubt cake and coffee are spewing out of their mouths all over the room. Then he says, "Peace be with you" (John 20:19).

It's inconceivable. Jesus is alive? After Jesus shows the disciples the wounds in his hands and his side, the disciples go crazy, whooping and hollering, probably hugging each other, wiping tears from their eyes. Jesus is alive! One small problem: Thomas wasn't there, and neither were you or I.

Now Thomas (called Didymus), one of the Twelve, was not with the disciples when Jesus came. So the other disciples told him, "We have seen the Lord!"

But he said to them, "Unless I see the nail marks in his hands and put my finger where the nails were, and put my hand into his side, I will not believe it."

John 20:24–25

Thomas heard the rumor from trusted friends that Jesus was alive and back from the dead. But he wouldn't believe it. It's quite possible that after Jesus' crucifixion Thomas didn't show up for the first get-together because he felt the meeting was pointless. He'd rather grieve alone. He had no desire to talk about what they might do next. No more get-togethers for him. Thomas was devastated.

But maybe he's thought it over, composed himself, taken a shower, shaved, and decided to visit his friends. After what they tell him, he probably wishes he had stayed home. He just knows they've lost it. He knows, like we do, that when someone dies they are not dead for a few days, they are *dead*, period. Thomas had believed that Jesus was the Messiah. But Messiahs aren't supposed to die; they're supposed to conquer! His hopes were shattered.

You know, it's probably not that he wouldn't believe but that he couldn't believe. Look again at Thomas's forceful yet sincere response. He says, "Unless I 'thrust' my fingers into his hands, and 'thrust' my hand into his side, you will never make me believe" (John 20:25, my paraphrase; the word *thrust* is taken from the Greek). Thomas had a determined unbelief.

I can understand that—I had a determined unbelief when I heard about a man washing his hands and face in sulfuric acid! Doc's "followers," his former students, kept stopping me in the hallway and telling me about this freaky thing he did. I had close friends telling me, "Jarrod, it's true; I swear to you he can do it. I've seen him do it in class." I just shook my head and laughed, "There is no way I will ever believe that! Well, actually, I take that back. Unless I see with my own eyes a spoon melt in that acid and watch him put his hands into that same acid, I will never believe it!"

What about you?

Like my unbelief in Doc and Thomas's unbelief in Jesus' resurrection, are you determined not to fully believe until all of your questions and doubts are answered? Let me ask it another way as you examine your heart: Are you sincere in your quest for truth? Or are you a skeptic of Jesus, as I was with Doc? Do you, like Thomas, crave belief? This makes all the difference. Jesus only has pity on those who seek him, crave him with their whole hearts, even in their doubts. Do you earnestly crave belief?

Evidence Demands a Verdict

A little over a week later, the disciples were hanging out again. Their doors were still locked because they were afraid that the Jewish religious authorities who had Jesus crucified would be coming after them next. But this time Thomas was with them.

> A week later his disciples were in the house again, and Thomas was with them. Though the doors were locked, Jesus came and stood among them and said, "Peace be with you!" Then he said to Thomas, "Put your finger here; see my hands. Reach out your hand and put it into my side. Stop doubting and believe."
>
> Thomas said to him, "My Lord and my God!"
>
> Then Jesus told him, "Because you have seen me, you have believed; blessed are those who have not seen and yet have believed."
>
> John 20:26–29

Again Jesus, in his unique way, shows up and says, "Peace be with you." No doubt the disciples, and especially Thomas, needed peace. Hanging out in a locked room when someone who was dead keeps popping up on the scene is definitely cause for a clean pair of boxers, as well as peace.

Just as we would move toward a hurting friend in a crowded funeral home, Jesus makes his move toward Thomas. Jesus repeats nearly word for word everything Thomas mentioned earlier. He invites Thomas to do what he needed to do in order to satisfy his craving for belief. Jesus says, "Thomas, here you go, look at my hands," and pulling his garment back says, "There you go, Thomas. Thrust your hand into my side if you need to. Start believing now, Thomas."

Thomas, confronted with the evidence, cries out, "My Lord and my God!" (v. 28). Thomas was a Jew. Remember Jesus' confrontation with the Jews back in John 8? Jews didn't believe Jesus was the Messiah they were waiting for. So for Thomas, a skeptic and a Jew, to cry out such words—words that declared Jesus not just Messiah but Lord and God—was absolutely staggering.

Thomas professes his belief, and then Jesus says: "Because you have seen me, you have believed" (v. 29 NASB). Jesus makes the point that Thomas believed because he saw. Jesus is not condemning Thomas. Thomas is simply privileged. His belief gets anchored to sight. We don't always necessarily have physical proof. For us, instead of sight bringing belief, belief now brings sight. In God's economy of things, we are the more privileged ones! Jesus looked ahead to you and me in that moment with Thomas and declared us "blessed." He said, "Blessed are those who have not seen and yet have believed" (v. 29). This is the greatest encouragement for those who embrace Christ by faith.

Back to Doc and the sulfuric acid for a minute. I had been determined to seek Doc out to get to the crux of the claims I was hearing about this sulfuric acid thing. A few nights later everything came full circle. The claims from his "followers" and finally the proof of the video confronted my unbelief with a call to respond. The evidence demanded a verdict. My verdict? I believed. In this case, all that belief did was acknowledge that sure enough, Doc was bizarre. But in the case of Thomas, his belief in Jesus was the cry of one who, when confronted with the proof, declared Jesus as Savior and Lord.

Do you believe? What kind of evidence do you need? How much evidence will it take? Here's the deal: no amount of evidence will ever truly scratch away your skeptical itch. God left a gap that must be crossed by faith. Why? Only faith pleases God.

> Without faith it is impossible to please God, for anyone who comes to him must believe that he exists and that he rewards those who earnestly seek him.
>
> Hebrews 11:6

God doesn't say he rewards those who believe the evidence; rather, he rewards those who earnestly seek him by faith. As Jesus said, "Blessed are those who have not seen and yet have believed" (John 20:29).

To Believe or Not to Believe

By God's great grace, he mercifully confronts us with convincing evidence. Though we weren't there with Thomas when he personally saw Jesus alive from death, John pens it (as an eyewitness) so that we will know Thomas's experience and then, like Thomas, believe! Look at the verses that are the climax of the entire book of John:

> Therefore many other signs Jesus also performed in the presence of the disciples, which are not written in this book; but these have been written so that you may believe that Jesus is the Christ, the Son of God; and that believing you may have life in His name.
>
> John 20:30–31 NASB

"It all comes down to this," John says. "I've poured out my heart by writing what I saw with my own eyes. I've poured my heart out so that you will believe and have life in Jesus' name!"

John mentions other signs that Jesus performed in the presence of his disciples. Why? Jesus was leaving the key to eternal life, the backward life, in the hands of these men. Their witness to Jesus' resurrection and his many miracles was to play a colossal role in the faith of everyone who embraces Jesus as their Lord and Savior since that time two thousand years ago.

Jesus' Identical Twin Brother?

I started to leave this out but couldn't resist including it. William Lane Craig tells the story of his debate with a professor from the University of California, Irvine, on the historical accuracy of Jesus' resurrection. Craig presented many of the facts I've shared with you in this chapter, which the professor couldn't refute.[1] Craig shares how the professor was grasping at straws to explain away the historical facts of Jesus' resurrection:

> So he argued that Jesus had an unknown, identical twin brother who had been separated from Him at birth, came back to Jerusalem just at the time of the crucifixion, stole Jesus' body out of the grave, and presented himself to the disciples, who mistakenly inferred that Jesus was risen from the dead! This theory shows what desperate lengths skeptics must go in order to deny the [historical facts] of the resurrection of Jesus.[2]

Need I add anything else?

Jesus: A Ghost from the Grave?

Have we misunderstood? I mean, was Jesus' resurrection meant to be taken in a spiritual, ghostly sense rather than a physical sense? Was the resurrected Jesus just a vision or hallucination of the women and the rest of the disciples, and even Thomas?

Didn't Thomas put his fingers into Jesus' nail-scarred hands and then into the scar in his side? You can't do that with a spirit, or a vision, or a hallucination. Jesus was physically alive from the dead.

Luke's account provides further details about the physical appearance of Jesus as he appeared to the disciples not as a spirit nor a vision or hallucination:

> But they were startled and frightened and thought that they were seeing a spirit. And He said to them, "Why are you troubled, and why do doubts arise in your hearts? See My hands and My feet, that it is I Myself; touch Me and see, for a spirit does not have flesh and bones as you see that I have."
>
> Luke 24:37–39 NASB

Remember John's account of Thomas's encounter with Jesus? Now look at one of his later writings:

> What was from the beginning, what we have *heard*, what we have *seen* with our eyes, what we have *looked at* and *touched* with our hands, concerning the Word of Life—and the life was manifested, and we have *seen* and testify and proclaim to you the eternal life, which was with the Father and was manifested to us—what we have *seen* and *heard* we proclaim to you also, so that you too may have fellowship with us; and indeed our fellowship is with the Father, and with His Son Jesus Christ. These things we write, so that our joy may be made complete.
>
> 1 John 1:1–4 NASB, emphasis added

In the Greek, which John originally wrote in, "looked at" literally means "scrutinized," which means "to examine closely; to look at very carefully; to inspect closely."[3] Picture it: John and the other disciples, with open mouths and speechless awe, inspecting Jesus' hands, cupping his face, feeling his beard and hair. On their knees before him, they touch and caress his feet, hardly able to take in the truth that he has risen from the dead. John is saying, "Read this! I am testifying and proclaiming this to you! I have written these things to you out of our joy, the joy in sharing this world-shaking truth with you!"

Can I Get a Show of Hands?

The apostle Paul now gets in on the deal. Three years after Jesus rocked Paul's world on the Damascus road (see Acts 9), Paul went to Peter and James to hear firsthand their eyewitness account of Jesus' resurrection (Gal. 1:18–19). Here is Paul's report, not only to the church at Corinth but to you and me:

> For I delivered to you as of first importance what I also received, that Christ died for our sins according to the Scriptures, and that He was buried, and that He was raised on the third day according to the Scriptures . . . and that *He appeared to more than five hundred brethren at one time, most of whom remain until now*, but some have fallen asleep [died]; *then He appeared to James*, then to all the apostles; and last of all, as to one untimely born, He appeared to me also.
>
> 1 Corinthians 15:3–8 NASB, emphasis added

Paul has done his investigation. He is now convinced beyond all doubt. He's so convinced that he's telling people to check it out for themselves: "I'm telling you, Jesus showed up and talked to more than five hundred people after he came alive from the dead. Most of them who saw him face to face are still around. If you don't believe me, call a few of them up, treat 'em to coffee at Starbucks, and they'll tell you everything!"

More than five hundred people saw Jesus physically alive after he was declared dead and gone. Most of them were still alive when Paul wrote those words. Wouldn't it be amazing to have the five hundred or so people still alive to meet in an auditorium and for a skeptic to grab a mic and say, "Okay, who in here saw Jesus alive from the dead? Now, I'm not talking about a vision, but who actually saw him physically alive from the dead? Can I get a show of hands?" Then in an instant he'd feel the draft from five hundred hands thrown up into the air!

Paul also says that Jesus appeared to James. James was Jesus' brother. Throughout Jesus' life, James and Jesus' other brothers didn't believe for a second that Jesus was the Son of God, or God, or any kind of Messiah or Savior. Actually James and many others thought Jesus had gone psycho with his claims. James was not a believer (Mark 3:21; John 7:5).

Flip the pages from the book of John to Acts 21. You'll discover James, the brother of Jesus, is the head of the very first Christian church in Jerusalem. How could this be? He once thought Jesus was a lunatic! But wait, there's more. James was also stoned to death thirty years later because of his faith in Jesus. What happened to James? What made him finally believe? Well, Paul tells you, "Then he [Jesus] appeared to James" (1 Cor. 15:7).

I can just imagine my sister Tyree's response if I was going around getting people to follow me, declaring that I was the Son of God, preaching that I could forgive sin, claiming that I would rise from the dead. My sister loves me very much. But I'm telling you, that would be more than she could handle. No doubt, even though she loved me, and out of great pain and embarrassment for me, she would do everything in her power to get me off the streets and into a psychiatric ward. She would plead with people to ignore my words and be merciful to me.

On the flip side, what would it take for my sister to truly believe what I claimed? What would cause her to do a "180" from her pity for me to going to her death testifying that I was who I said I was like James did about Jesus? It would take a hole in the ground containing an empty casket with the top ripped off, and then an "I'm baaaaack . . ." as I physically appeared face-to-face with her in my resurrection glory. The report would read, "Then he appeared to Tyree."

Where's the DVD?

Eleven days after his resurrection, Jesus stood before Thomas, who proclaimed, "My Lord and my God!" (John 20:28). There is no DVD of Jesus' resurrection like the videotape I saw about Doc. But think of all the testimonies from John, Paul, Matthew, Mark,

Peter, James, and more than five hundred people that day. John himself says over and over again, "I've written, I've proclaimed, I've testified, it's true! Jesus rose from the dead!" That's why he ends Thomas's story with the greatest invitation on the planet: "These [things] are written that you may believe that Jesus is the Christ, the Son of God, and that believing you may have life in His name" (John 20:31 NKJV).

A few years ago I met a young businessman from Chicago who was about thirty years old, newly married, and a former atheist. He was in West Virginia with a church group, serving to help the poor. On a van ride I asked him about his belief in Jesus. I asked him, "What convinced you?" He shared that he had wrestled with many different claims of Christianity, but the deciding factor was Jesus. He said, "One day it just hit me, and I realized that if Jesus rose from the dead, he is who he said he was. That was the ultimate; that changed everything. So I believed and trusted in Jesus as my Savior. Now, a year later, I am spending my vacation here in West Virginia repairing homes for the poor and telling people about Jesus."

Spending a vacation repairing homes for the poor and telling people about Jesus? Is it just me or does that sound . . . *backward*? All this talk about the resurrection of Jesus is not just facts of faith. It's life ruining. Seriously, you could go from being a comfortable skeptic, earning a nice living for *yourself* and enjoying big vacations for *yourself*, to giving your comfort, your money, your time, even your life away serving God and others. Oh yes, it is backward. But it's the life you were created to live. The backward life is a life resurrected from self, alive to God and others.

10

The Power of a Touch

There is another way to live.

actor Matt Damon

I remember when I was nine years old, standing in the front yard of my grandmother's house throwing a baseball with my best friend, Kirk. Right in front of my eyes, my dog was hit by a car on the highway. I was devastated. I ran inside and telephoned my mom, barely able to get out a word because I was crying so hard. When I hung up the phone, my best friend walked up to me, hugged me tight, and cried with me. We were only nine years old, but I remember it like it was nine minutes ago.

The power of a touch. The touch of a mother's hand to her child's face. The kiss of a husband's lips on his wife's cheek. The hug of a best friend to a little boy who just lost his dog. When words won't do, a touch says it all.

If a human touch is so powerful, imagine the touch of God. His touch is lifesaving and life changing. It's as if with his touch, the old you dies and a new you happens.

If anyone is in Christ, he is a new creation; the old has gone, the new has come!

2 Corinthians 5:17

See what happens to two blind beggars when they are "touched" by Jesus.

As Jesus and his disciples were leaving Jericho, a large crowd followed him. Two blind men were sitting by the roadside, and when they heard Jesus was going by, they shouted, "Lord, Son of David, have mercy on us!"

The crowd rebuked them and told them to be quiet, but they shouted all the louder, "Lord, Son of David, have mercy on us!"

Jesus stopped and called them. "What do you want me to do for you?" he asked.

"Lord," they answered, "we want our sight."

Matthew 20:29–33

Moved with compassion, Jesus touched their eyes; and immediately they regained their sight and followed Him.

Matthew 20:34 NASB

Jesus' touch is so powerful that it takes a self-absorbed, wayward life and makes it a gloriously ruined, backward life.

One thing you can't deny from this story about these blind beggars: they were begging for their sight desperately. "Desperate" seems to be an appropriate description of many people today, perhaps including you too. Much of the world seems desperate—looking for answers anywhere and everywhere, from extreme body makeovers to extreme home makeovers. People are desperately seeking a touch of compassion from anyone who might understand. Does that touch a nerve with you? It does for me too.

Desperation is a place where you're near rock bottom. As the old saying goes, once you've hit rock bottom, there's nowhere to look but up. Desperation is not such a bad place if you think backward—

because it's the exact place where you meet God. Author Philip Yancey put it this way: "We are all desperate, and that is in fact the only state appropriate to a human being who wants to know God."[1]

So what are you desperate for? The weekend? A paycheck? A new career? A new car? A vacation? Marriage? Are you desperate for answers? Hope? Relief? Peace?

However you label it, at some level, everyone is desperate—desperate to satisfy a longing, a heart's desire. Philosopher George Bernard Shaw wrote that there were two great tragedies in life: one is to lose your heart's desire. The other is to gain it.[2]

My parents had a dog named Sumo. He was a Chinese pug (yeah, I know, sumo is Japanese). This was one ugly dog, friend. He had a barrel-like body, no neck, and a little head with a flat face and bulging eyes. But, he was so ugly that he was cute, kind of like Gollum in Lord of the Rings.

Sumo loved to chase his tail. He would tune everything out, even his favorite jelly beans, desperate to catch his tail. His heart's desire was his tail.

Well, one day it happened. Don't ask me how, but he did it. He reached his "heart's desire." But what was it? Just a tail! How bummed out do you think he was?

It's no different with us. We tire ourselves out physically, relationally, mentally, emotionally, and spiritually. We run around in circles seeking to find the ultimate "self," people's approval, and things of this world. Then, if or when we reach it, we discover it's only a tail.

Matt Damon was interviewed by Dotson Rader of *Parade* magazine about his journey to fame. As Damon reflected upon winning the Oscar for his screenwriting role in *Good Will Hunting*, he said, "I remember the night of the Academy Awards and going home after having been given this great prize that was supposed to make me happy. I was alone, and I looked at this thing, and I heard myself say, almost out loud, 'Thank God I didn't screw over anybody for this, because it wouldn't have been worth it.'"[3] No wonder Damon said, "There is another way to live." He caught fame and discovered it was only a tail.

Some of Jesus' disciples entered into the chase too. In Matthew 20:18–19, Jesus told his disciples, "We are going up to Jerusalem, and the Son of Man will be betrayed to the chief priests and the teachers of the law. They will condemn him to death and will turn him over to the Gentiles to be mocked and flogged and crucified. On the third day he will be raised to life."

If I had been one of the disciples Jesus was talking to, I would have begged for an explanation. I would have told him that I would never allow such a thing to happen to him. I would have pleaded with him not to go to Jerusalem, to go pray about it some more or something along those lines. I would have expected this from his disciples. But instead I see something that lets the proverbial air out of the bag:

> Then the mother of Zebedee's sons came to Jesus with her sons and, kneeling down, asked a favor of him.
>
> "What is it you want?" he asked.
>
> She said, "Grant that one of these two sons of mine may sit at your right and the other at your left in your kingdom."
>
> Matthew 20:20–21

What? Jesus had just poured out his heart about the gruesome death he was facing in a few days. Instead of concern and heartbreak, he got two disciples getting their mommy to ask him to give them a "shout-out" when he got to heaven. They wanted to sit with him where all eyes would fall on them. Jesus had just shared that he was headed to a butchering on the cross, and these disciples were more concerned about their popularity and positions. This reminds me of . . . me. The disciples lost touch with their desperation for Jesus, like I so often do. After three years with Jesus, the disciples no doubt became too familiar with him. They slipped into the "Jesus is my homeboy" fan club. They were more in tune with following the "large crowd" behind Jesus than with intimacy with Jesus. They fell into the rhythm of tail-chasing rather than Jesus-following. At the same time, two other men were so desperate that they were shouting over the crowd for Jesus, not fitting into the crowd.

The blind beggars knew there must be another way to live. They were desperate—desperate for their sight, desperate for their lives, sick of chasing their tails. They didn't shout for Jesus to give them money. They didn't shout for Jesus to help them. They didn't shout for Jesus to "bless" them. They didn't shout for Jesus to give them popularity and position. They shouted, "Lord . . . have mercy on us!" (Matt. 20:30–31).

Mercy is a word that gets Jesus' attention. It's a word that comes off the lips of one who sees his darkness, his emptiness, his desperation. That's exactly where these men were—in darkness, in need, and desperate. They were at their wits' end. They knew there must be more. Ever been there?

You try to ignore it as you play church every Sunday. You whisper it as you wash the dishes. You sense it as you drop your kids off at school. You pray it as you leave the party. *"There must be more."* You feel it after the one-night stand. You ponder it as you lie down in bed at night. You carry it like lead as you head out of town for business. You're numb with it even as you get the raise you've worked so hard for. You were haunted by it when you were single, and you're still haunted now that you're married. You wake up in the morning and it nauseates you. *"There must be more."* And like the blind men, you're begging, desperate, sick and tired of chasing your tail.

If you're begging for more to life, then what is blinding you—the pursuit of happiness, success, self-empowerment? Or is it anger, jealousy, bitterness, anxiety? The blind men were so desperate that they didn't let their blindness control them anymore. They heard hope walking by, and they wanted to see. They sensed God was near, and they wanted a touch. They cried out for Jesus.

The blind men had another problem. There was a crowd yelling at them to shut up and leave Jesus alone: "The crowd rebuked them and told them to be quiet" (Matt. 20:31).

Who is your "crowd"? Who or what is keeping you from Jesus? Self-deception? The echo of guilt over prior mistakes, or "the mistake," you've made in your life? The pounding anger you've harbored for years?

It's time to ignore the crowd, friend. It's time to plug your ears to the voices of self-pity. It's time to see you have just as many faults as the next guy. It's time for you to embrace a merciful friend—Jesus—and become a merciful friend.

That's what the blind beggars did: "The crowd rebuked them and told them to be quiet, but they shouted all the louder, 'Lord . . . have mercy on us!'" (Matt. 20:31). They didn't let their blindness get in the way anymore. They didn't let the crowd hush them anymore. They were sick of their old life of darkness. They were sick of being desperate. They were sick of chasing their tails. They ignored the crowd and "shouted all the louder" for mercy.

And God heard, for "he rewards those who earnestly seek him" (Heb. 11:6).

When you earnestly cry out for Jesus like the blind beggars, he will hear. It may still be dark for a while, circumstances might not change the way you want, and you may *feel* that your prayer rolled off your lips and onto the floor. But I promise you—no, God promises you—he hears. "'You will seek me and find me when you seek me with all your heart. I will be found by you,' declares the LORD" (Jer. 29:13–14).

When I was seventeen years old, I went caving with my church youth group. We went two hours deep into a cave. It was the real deal. We wore hard hats, carried garbage bags with our clothes and sleeping bags, and used a portable toilet—a bucket behind a sheet. I have never been so miserable in all my life. Caves, poopy buckets, and a bunch of fourteen- through seventeen-year-olds do not get along well.

The agenda was to hike deep into this cave and spend the night—in the cave! Finally we got to a part of the cave where I could almost straighten up and stretch my back. We all agreed this would be where we would crash for the night. In an effort to get away from those who made nighttime bodily noises with their mouths and, well, other parts of the human anatomy, some friends and I crawled up into a narrow crevice to sleep. We crawled into a space where the roof was only two feet from our faces when we were lying down. I pushed my sleeping bag into the crevice and lay down with my helmet light still on. I thought, *I just might freak out.* I took deep breaths, hoping I would make it through the night. I finally got the nerve to shut off my light. *Go to happy place, go to happy place,* I consoled myself.

Halfway through the night I had a dream that everyone left me behind. I woke up with my heart beating out of my chest. I couldn't see my hand in front of my face, it was so dark. "Hello?" I said. There was no response. "Bob?" I said (Bob was my youth minister). Again, no response. Hyperventilating, I tried to sit up, still unable to see or hear anything, and I lost it. I started screaming like a seven-year-old little girl—"BOB! BOB! BOB!" Funny thing is that Bob was calling back to me at the same time. But I couldn't hear him. I was so focused on the dark. Then I just ran out of gas, I guess. I stopped and became still. It was then that I heard Bob saying, "Jarrod, Jarrod, I'm here. I'm right here."

Like the blind men, we "cry out" in our darkness and even at our darkness. But what the blind men cried out for was mercy. *Mercy* is a word that gets Jesus' attention. Your cry for mercy stops God on a dime and focuses his heart on you. So, if you must, cry out, but cry out for mercy. Jesus will stop, hear, and answer, "I'm here for you. I'm right here for you." You just have to listen.

I didn't hear Bob calling back to me because of my unending shouts. I didn't hear him, that is, until I stopped and listened. The blind men only heard Jesus when they ceased shouting. You might need to do the same. Cease shouting and start listening.

When we are hurting, afraid, in the dark, we become impatient and sometimes irrational. We want instant answers, direction, peace, healing, provision, and God's attention. Little do we know that Jesus is in our very presence, and we in his. We just need to be still and listen for a change. We need to settle down, take deep breaths, close our eyes, meditate on him, and wait for his words and his touch.

So after the beggars stopped shouting, they heard Jesus respond, "What do you want me to do for you?" (Matt. 20:32).

I consider myself a disciple of Jesus. But I want to be like the blind men. I never want to be just a member of Jesus' fan club. I don't want Jesus as my homeboy. I want him as my Savior. I want to be a man in touch with my blindness without Jesus, my need for mercy through Jesus, and my desperate everyday need for Jesus. What about you?

On another note, I am amazed that Jesus not only heard the blind men but also stopped for them. Jesus had left the crowds of Jericho, headed for a cross in Jerusalem. He was on his death march to die for the sins of the world. Don't you think Jesus might have been a little preoccupied with what was about to happen instead of paying attention to two aggravating blind people? The people might have expected the king of the world to say: "Somebody get these bums away from me! Don't they know who they're talking to? I am the Messiah. I'm the Savior. I don't have the time or energy for these guys. I've got a cross to think about. They're messing up my focus."

But Jesus is backward. He does just the opposite of what might be expected. He stops for those who desperately cry out for mercy. He pauses for those who have not lost touch with their intense need for him. He looked at two of his closest disciples who wanted the spotlight in heaven and said, "You don't know what you're talking about." He looked at the blind men and was "moved with compassion" (Matt. 20:34 NASB). In the original Greek language of the Bible, *compassion* means "a wrenching in the guts." Jesus was intensely moved, saddened, and brokenhearted over the despair of these men. This gives us another clue to the backward life. It's not a life that loves and serves others out of a sense of responsibility or duty. It's a life of compassion, a life that is brokenhearted for people who are desperate and hopeless.

A few years ago, I got an emergency phone call from my mother about the dad of one of my best friends. This was one of those friends who was like an adopted member of my family, as I was of his family. We were in the church nursery together, we played Little League ball together, and we were roommates after college.

The tragic news was that his dad had committed suicide. Now, I hadn't seen or talked to my friend since I'd been in his wedding a year earlier. I got in my car for the hour-long drive to his family home where I knew he would be. Honestly, I was numb. I don't know if I was in shock or just a jerk, but I didn't feel much. Instead of thinking of my friend and his family, I was thinking, "I haven't seen or talked to him in a year, and I'm just going to show up unannounced? What do I say? What do I do? What will he think?"

Suddenly I realized how selfish I was, thinking more about me in this situation than about the family. So I began to pray. My prayer was something like, "Lord, I'm numb. How do *you* feel about their tragedy? How do *you* feel about what my friend and his family are going through? Lord, please, let me feel what you feel."

As I prayed, memories began to pour into my heart about my friend and his family. My eyes filled with tears—the friend who had hugged me and cried with me when my dog was killed by a car, Kirk, was the very friend I was on my way to see.

I finally arrived at his parents' home. As I turned in to the driveway, I saw Kirk standing alone at the back corner of the house. As I pulled up beside him and turned off the car, our eyes met. In that instant I saw such despair, confusion, pain. He was blindsided by his father's death, begging for answers. I got out of the car. I walked toward him and he toward me. Then we embraced. As he cried on my shoulder, I cried my eyes out for him.

Compassion. I cried because I deeply hurt for my friend. I cried because compassion for him and his family overwhelmed me. That kind of compassion was not of me; it was the compassion of Jesus. I never spoke a word to Kirk. Why? Words wouldn't do. They just wouldn't do. Kirk needed more than words—he needed a touch.

"Moved with compassion, Jesus touched their eyes" (Matt. 20:34). Jesus was so brokenhearted with compassion for the blind beggars that he never said a word. Words wouldn't do, so he touched them, and they were made whole. "Immediately they received their sight and followed him" (v. 34).

When these blind men were touched by Jesus, they were made new, healed not only on the outside but on the inside. Jesus gave them physical sight and spiritual sight. Their response? They followed him.

Bye-bye "old" and hello "new!" When you are truly touched by the Savior Jesus, you can't help but follow him. To live for Jesus is to live backward. This can't happen apart from being first loved by God and then loving God with all your heart, mind, soul, and strength. The love of the Father for Jesus and the love of Jesus for his Father and others is what made Jesus stop and touch the blind beggars. Now the blind beggars will follow Jesus and be the touch of Jesus by loving the God they're made for and living the life they're meant for—a life of loving other desperate people.

Become like the blind beggars:

- **Humble yourself.** Draw near to the Jesus of mercy, and he will mercifully draw near to you. The backward life is a life of humility before God and others.
- **Ignore the crowd.** Ignore your "self" and turn to your Lord. Dare to be set apart. Ignore the seduction of the world. No matter how good it looks, it's only pocket change.
- **Listen for his voice.** When you can't see the hand of God around you, trust God's merciful heart for you.
- **Embrace his touch.** If you haven't already, embrace the touch of Christ by faith and be saved from your sin and self and an

eternity apart from the God you're made for. Then embrace Jesus' touch through his church and through worship.

- **Follow him.** Become his touch to the world. Live backward to the world. Be different from the world. Love God with all your might. Love others as yourself. Deny yourself, carry your cross, and follow Jesus (Luke 9:23).

The power of a touch: a gentle touch from your father and you're encouraged; a caring touch from your mother and you're consoled; a loving touch from a friend and you're comforted; a compassionate touch from Jesus and you're ruined—gloriously ruined. Then a Jesus touch through you to a broken world and you're hooked . . . on the backward life.

11

Backward Loving

It's hard to care deeply for something that might turn on you and eat you.

Peter Benchley, author of Jaws

My dad has aged in appearance in the last few years. He has a head full of gray hair and a gray beard to show for it. He's had a heart attack and triple bypass heart surgery at the age of forty-nine to thank for it. Although he jokes about his aged appearance, I can tell it bothers him a bit.

Not too long ago, Dad was flipping through magazines as he awaited his turn for a haircut at the barber shop he's been frequenting for years. A teenage kid with Down's syndrome had just stepped out of the chair with his new "do" and was making his rounds hugging the hairstylists. As he turned to make his way out the door, his eyes connected with Dad's. Then up to Dad—a stranger—he walked, opened his arms wide, and affectionately purred, "Paaawpaaaw." I could hardly breathe from laughing when Dad told me the story.

Dad would say, tongue in cheek, that that was the most "love" he'd received in a long time. It's funny to hear him playfully complain about how his granddaughter, my niece Mattie, only pays attention to him when she wants money, a new toy, or chocolate ice cream that her mom said she couldn't have. He even pulls the family dog into it, saying that the only attention he ever gets from her is when she wants him to play fetch with the doggy Frisbee or scratch her belly. Thinking back on my teenage years, I can still hear him grumble, "The only time you and your sister ever acknowledge me is when you need money or my permission to do something."

Sometimes jokingly, sometimes truthfully, Dad growls about how those he loves only love him when they can get something from him. I'd bet my dad voices the feeling of most dads in America and perhaps of people in most relationships in the world today. Most of us enter into relationships not because we desire to give to a person but because of what we receive from him or her.

Either by default or intentionally, we enter into relationships with lurking thoughts of how the person can benefit us, what they can do for us, what they might give us, or how they might help us: "Yes! She might introduce *me* to her brother; he might get *me* free tickets to the concert; she will be a great contact for getting *me* the job; he's the ticket for getting *me* the gigs."

Often we weigh the value of a relationship based on its tangible benefits—the love, the self-esteem, the attention, or the stuff the other person gives us. It's true. I'm guilty of it. You're guilty of it. I'm not proud of it. I don't like it. I fight it and pray against it. Yet those ulterior motives shadow every relationship I have, from my grandmother to my best friend to my wife.

Reflect on your relationships for just a moment: Is this how you measure your relationships—based on what the person might be able to do for you?

An Impossible Love Made Possible

Backward living and backward loving begin with embracing God's love and pursuing God's heart by faith. As this love affair grows, we love God, not self, with everything we have (see Mark 12:30). This love spills over onto others more and more (see Mark 12:31).

Without the powerful love of God flowing through us, there's no way we can truly love others. God's love first impassions backward living in us. God's love through us and our love for him births backward loving from us.

The Big Three

Backward loving doesn't mean blindly loving. It means loving people despite their faults. In other words, you see their faults, you conclude there is nothing you can do to change them, but you love them anyway. If you see they have a need, you will meet it. This is tough, sometimes impossible, without God loving through us. Even so, we still have to consciously surrender to his love and abandon "self" to love others the way he designed us to.

Here are three big questions we have to answer as we try to scale this seemingly unconquerable mountain of loving others without regard to self.

Why should I love others?
How do I love others?
What's holding me back from loving others?

The answers to these questions give us freedom to sail the life we're meant to live and discover the love we're meant to give.

Why Should I Love Others?

People Are Valuable and Last Forever

God calls us to love others as much as we love ourselves because people are created in his image (Gen. 1:27), and personally "knit" by God and described by God through the psalmist as "fearfully and wonderfully made" (Ps. 139:13–14). Scripture also tells us that people are lost, like sheep without a shepherd (Jer. 50:6), and that Jesus personally came to seek those who are lost (Luke 19:10).

In Luke 15, Jesus compares a lost person to a lost sheep, a lost coin, and a lost son. The shepherd who lost one of his sheep out of the fold of one hundred leaves them all to go after the one lost sheep. When he finds it, he calls his friends and throws a party. The woman who lost one of her ten silver coins turns her house upside down looking for it. When she finds it, she also calls her friends to throw a party. The father who lost his son when his son took all his inheritance and left home to pursue a party lifestyle hiked up his robe and ran to his son with open arms when the son returned home. The father gave his son a new ring and coat and called all his friends and family together to—you guessed it—throw a party. Jesus uses all of this imagery to drive home the point that people are valuable.

While in grad school I immersed myself in reading and studying. Unless I was at church or out of town for speaking engagements, I wasn't spending any time with other people. A fellow student and I began meeting for lunch every now and then, going to coffee shops to study. She asked me one day, "Jarrod, I hardly ever see you around outside of class. Do you have any friends? Do you ever do anything besides study?" I answered, "Not really. I've got too much on my plate. I don't have time to hang out much." To which she replied, "Don't ever forget, Jarrod—tasks don't last forever, people do."

Tasks don't last forever, people do—her statement nailed me. It haunted me as I blasted through my days checking off my to-do lists without investing in anyone else's life. She was so right.

Think about it. Only two things last forever on this earth: (1) God's Word and (2) people. Every person on earth—past, present, and future—will live forever . . . somewhere. Our souls are eternal as God is eternal. We're created in his image. That's why the apostle John said that hating someone is the same as murdering someone in God's eyes:

> Anyone who hates his brother is a murderer, and you know that no murderer has eternal life in him.
>
> 1 John 3:15

Nothing can "murder," or poison, souls like our words. Our words can be weapons of mass destruction, demolishing people created in God's image. The apostle James said:

> All kinds of animals, birds, reptiles and creatures of the sea are being tamed and have been tamed by man, but no man can tame the tongue. It is a restless evil, full of deadly poison.
>
> James 3:7–8

We often use words to show off our sense of humor at someone else's expense. We learn this at a young age. When my niece, Mattie, was three years old, we were all sitting at my parents' table for breakfast on a Saturday morning. I looked up from my grits and noticed that Mattie was giving me the "stink eye." I froze, raised my eyebrows, and said, "Uh, what is it, Mattie?"

She smiled from ear to ear and bobbed her head side to side as she sang a little jingle to me: "Peanut butter . . . and jelly, JJ's got a . . . fat belly!" Three years old and she's already singing a song—that rhymes, mind you—about my body's problem areas.

Without thinking, I bellowed back, "Peanut butter . . . and bread, Mattie's got a . . . fat head."

But she didn't take it as a joke. She was only three years old, for crying out loud.

I apologized, told her I was only playing, and hoped I didn't scar her for life. She is older now, and I think she is okay so far.

Although this is a very tame example, people spew out and receive much more victimizing words every day. One person's laughter is another person's terror. Beware of launching words of mass destruction.

It's Love for God Gone Public

We must also love others because loving them is proof of our love for God. Loving others is the stage on which the backward life is displayed. If we lack love for one person or for many, or if our only goal is to use people to further our own agendas, then according to Scripture, we are liars if we say we love God.

> We know that we have passed from death to life, because we love our brothers. Anyone who does not love remains in death. . . . If anyone says, "I love God," yet hates his brother, he is a liar. For anyone who does not love his brother, whom he has seen, cannot love God, whom he has not seen.
>
> 1 John 3:14; 4:20

God does not mess around. People are valuable to him. They are created in his image. He passionately loves people. He loves so much that he died for us on a cross through his Son Jesus. That's his backward love in action. He expects no less from us. He wants our backward love in action—loving others by taking up his cross, crucifying ourselves, and giving our lives away.

God Says So

Finally, even if none of the other reasons compute, we love others for one ultimate reason: God says so. And that's enough.

> And he has given us this command: Whoever loves God must also love his brother.
>
> 1 John 4:21

How Do I Love Others?

Deeply

First Peter 4:8 says, "Love each other deeply." The Greek word for "deeply" is heavy with meaning. It means, "at full stretch; an intense strain like the taut muscles of an athlete straining to win the race."[1]

I still remember the after-practice sprints from my basketball days at Samford University. The coaches would put a very short countdown on the clock and make us run from sideline to sideline before the buzzer went off. And if someone didn't make it in time, the whole team would run again. Talk about an intense strain! My leg muscles felt like fire and burned with fatigue; my stomach did flips as I felt my lunch gurgling up toward my mouth; and often I had to dive over the sideline at full stretch to beat the buzzer. I ache even now just thinking about it.

This is the picture of loving others deeply. We're to love at full stretch and with an intense strain. We're to love when we're sick of loving and not getting anything in return. We're to love even when we think we can't love anymore. We're to love when everything in us and everything around us screams "give up!" We're to love even when it hurts.

Unfortunately, we seem to have to love this way the majority of the time. Our "self" constantly cries for attention and comfort. And when our love is betrayed or not returned, we want to chuck the whole "love others" thing like a 1980s Atari.

Devotedly

"Be devoted to one another in brotherly love," says Paul in Romans 12:10. Backward loving is loving others with devotion. The kind of devotion Scripture speaks of is family devotion—not just for our families but for all people as if they were our family.

One Monday afternoon during my second year of seminary, I got a call from my sister. I could tell she was excited, but I had no idea why. My sister had gotten divorced two years prior, but for the past year or so she had been growing closer to a very special man in her life. She said, "Jarrod, guess what? I'm getting married!"

"What?!" I asked with excitement and shock. "Oh my gosh, when is the big day?"

She answered, "This Saturday!"

After regaining consciousness and crawling over to a chair, my first thought was, "What in the world? Doesn't she know I've got a life? I've got classes to attend, papers to write, midterms to study for. I have ministry engagements coming up, and I've got to prepare. Five days notice she gives me . . ." Again, all about me.

When I finished sulking, I took a deep breath, called Southwest Airlines, and booked a flight to Birmingham, Alabama, for Friday afternoon. And I did it with pleasure and joy. I am devoted to her because I love her and because she is my sister. I dropped everything in the blink of an eye to have the honor of being there for her on her big day.

As backward as it may sound, this is the same kind of devotion that we're to give any person in our lives. Even though they are not family-related, we're to love them in that family-devoted kind of way—to drop everything to help them and support them, whether they need a hand to hold, a shoulder to cry on, a dollar to spend, or our best advice or just want to see our smiling face as they walk down the aisle the second time. Yep, it's definitely backward. But it's the life you're meant to live, and it's the love you're meant to give.

Sacrificially

As I travel around the country, I get a chance to meet many interesting people. I especially enjoy meeting and chatting with people from other countries. Somewhere in the conversation I'll toss in these two questions: "Is America what you expected it to be?" and "What about America has been the biggest letdown?"

The first question is almost always answered the same way. They expected America to be like MTV from coast to coast. Unfortunately for those looking forward to this, most of them ended up someplace like my home state of Alabama (which I love, by the way) or Idaho, discovering an America more like the Weather Channel.

For the second question I've often received answers that convicted me but didn't surprise me. I specifically remember talking to a guy from El Salvador, if memory serves correctly. He said his biggest letdown about America was that "Americans seem to just look out for themselves. They only look out for number one. Even in family homes, kids only do for themselves, wives and husbands seem to do their own thing, even mothers and fathers. Americans just seem, well, selfish."

Sacrifice is a word that makes most of us cringe when we hear it, but it's part of the backward life equation.

Outdo one another in showing honor.

Romans 12:10 HCSB

Owe nothing to anyone except to love one another.

Romans 13:8 NASB

Do nothing out of rivalry or conceit, but in humility consider others as more important than yourselves. Everyone should look out not only for his own interests, but also for the interests of others.

Philippians 2:3–4 HCSB

Loving sacrificially, as Scripture reveals, is what backward loving and purposeful living is all about.

Sincerely

Paul says that we are also to love sincerely: "Love must be sincere" (Rom. 12:9). What exactly does it mean to love sincerely?

In ancient times, potters would make and bake jars, bowls, or dishes to use and to sell in the marketplace. Due to impurities in the clay, many times the pottery would have a crack, making it useless garbage. A cracked jar, pot, or bowl would be useless. But because of the money invested in the materials, the potter would try to cover up the cracks and holes with wax and finish it off with a coat of paint.

People were buying the jars and dishes to cook food and contain hot substances. Due to the heat, the wax would melt, exposing the corrupted jar or plate. Once the people became wise to the schemes of these potters, they took their business elsewhere. In an attempt to regain trust and increase business again, the potters abandoned their cheating ways and engraved a word on the bottom of the pottery as a seal of authenticity. The word engraved was *sincera*, which means "without wax."[2]

Sincera is the root word of our English word *sincerely*. So, for instance, every time I write an email or a letter and end it with "Sincerely, Jarrod," what I'm really saying is, "without wax, Jarrod." Although *sincera* is actually not the Greek word Paul uses, the meaning is still the same. Loving sincerely, according to Paul, is loving without hypocrisy—"without wax."

Sincere loving is genuine love. It says, "I love you, neighbor, with no strings attached, with no underlying motives, with no phoniness." It's an honest and vulnerable love. If you love sincerely, you're saying, "I love you. There are no cracks in my love for you. I won't try to get anything out of you or take anything from you. I won't lie about anything to you or hide anything from you. I love you—warts and all. And I'm giving you all of me as a friend—warts and all. I won't hold anything back from you. It's a risk, I know. I'm setting myself up to get hurt. It doesn't matter. I'm made for this."

You might think this is the kind of love God intended just for marriage. On the contrary, sincere love is the love we are also meant to give to our neighbor. It's a love that risks and that could lead to heartbreak if rejected or betrayed. But if rejection or betrayal does come, we will not be ruined. Our "everything" is found in the God who first loved us, in the Jesus whom we love. Though we'll weep and ache, we are free from devastation because we put our faith in

Jesus, not another human being. Jesus is where we find our fountain of life, love, joy, and purpose.

Loving sincerely is so backward that our neighbor could see it as a green light to take advantage of us, steal from us, cheat us, or hurt us. That sounds kind of like what happened to Jesus, doesn't it? Sure, it's dangerous—it's backward.

What's Holding Me Back?

Self

When we think of what's holding us back from loving sincerely, it's not surprising that "self" has again slithered into the picture. The sin of self holds us back from loving others the way we're meant to love them.

Self shows up in loving ourselves so much that we won't dare step out to risk discomfort, intrusion, or heartache. It could be that we're too in love with our agendas, tasks, to-do lists, and Day-Timers. We may have been so hurt by others that we hold tightly to grudges and bitterness. We cling to self-pity.

Whatever issues we have, they all boil down to trusting self more than God, loving self more than others.

Fear

Peter Benchley, author of the novel *Jaws*, which was made into a hit movie, was interviewed by Bob Minzesheimer of *USA Today*. In the interview, Benchley discussed his fascination with and affection for sharks. Yet Benchley remarked, "It's hard to care deeply for something that might turn on you and eat you."[3]

Sounds like the danger that lurks in loving and caring for people, doesn't it? Benchley's statement hits the nail on the head when we think of giving our lives away and loving others in a vulnerable way. It's hard for us to care deeply for others because they might turn on us and hurt us deeply. Have you been "shark-bitten" yet? At speaking engagements I've asked people to raise their hands if their answer is yes. Every time, as far as I could see, every hand in the place was high in the air. What I say to them, I will say to you: it won't be the last time.

Backward loving makes us vulnerable to being hurt by the people we've entrusted with our hearts. The easy way out is to let fear control and protect us, but what a miserable life! A life with no risk is no life at all. A love with no risk is no love at all. If fear is on the throne of our lives, then Jesus is not. Paul says:

> For God did not give us a spirit of timidity, but a spirit of power, of love, and of self-discipline.
>
> 2 Timothy 1:7

Jesus never promised us safety and comfort. He promised that he would always love us and never abandon us. A risky life is a backward life. A risky love is a backward love.

Pain

I'll never forget the pain I felt years ago when the girl I wanted to marry told me she was in love with another guy and never wanted to see me again. For weeks after, I was physically sick from crying so hard. I moped around, unable to eat, laugh, or talk. I received tons of advice and encouragement from friends and family. But the words my dad hammered me with were the ones that finally hit home and jerked me out of my stupor.

I was standing outside, staring down my parents' long driveway, with tears streaming down my face and a deep aching in my gut. My dad saw me as he was making his rounds checking out the plants in the yard. He had already sat down with me many times, giving me gentle advice about how to deal with my loss. This time he bluntly said these electrifying words: "Jarrod, son, listen to me. You got burned. That's all there is to it. You got burned. Take it on the chin like a man and get on with your life." Nothing really that spiritual there, but God used those words to spur me on to healing, strength, and renewed joy.

I'm sure you can think of at least one time you've gotten burned or "shark-bitten." And I'm not talking about just by a past boyfriend or girlfriend. It may have been by a friend, co-worker, business partner, husband, wife, parent, or all the above. Sometimes that burn or shark bite can be so painful, so devastating, and so big that it becomes a god, affecting every part of our lives, controlling everything we do. It becomes so big, in fact, that it makes God about a millimeter tall in our lives, with about a thimbleful of power and love in our lives.

Pain can definitely hold us back. But this is where faith comes in. Faith in our great, powerful, sovereign, and good God is essential. He's the one who enables us to take "it" on the chin and move forward in faith. Through our Father's first love we keep on risking and loving, knowing that he will heal the burns, the bites, and the bruised chins that will come time and time again.

Love through the Hurt

Derek Redmond was headed toward the finish line in the 400-meter semifinal heat of the 1992 Olympic Games. Tragically, he suddenly popped a hamstring. Still, Derek hobbled around the Olympic stadium track the best he could, hoping to at least reach the finish line and finish the race. At the top of the stadium packed with 65,000 people, Derek's dad sat watching his son's struggle unfold. Finally, unable to take the sight any longer, Derek's dad bolted down flights of stairs and past security guards to get to his son on the track. After catching up with Derek, he put an arm around his son's waist, and together they did a three-legged hobble across the finish line.[4]

The reality is this: backward loving will lead to "popped hamstrings" as we love others. It may have already happened to you—betrayal, abandonment, ridicule. You've made up your mind. There is no way you will risk loving anyone—friend, stranger, lover, or foe—like that again. But friend, that is the easy way out. That is the selfish way out. Never forget that we're meant to love even when we pop a hamstring. We're meant to love even when it hurts. Welcome to Christianity. Jesus loved even when it hurt—all the way to the cross.

The glory of backward loving is that you don't do it on your own. When you pull a hamstring, there is a God in heaven, Father God, who will always run to meet you, put his arms around you, love you, and love through you all the way across the finish line.

12

The Backward Truth

So many right-wing Christians . . . so few lions.

popular anti-Christian T-shirt

A few years ago, while in Louisville, Kentucky, I walked with a few friends down a rowdy section of Bardstown Road. Our mission: share the gospel with anything that moved.

I approached a guy who looked like he was in his early twenties. A bit nervous, I introduced myself and told him that I was out sharing my faith in Jesus Christ. I asked if he would give me a few minutes to tell him about how Jesus saved my soul and how Jesus could do the same for him.

Immediately the guy said, "Ohhhh, okay, all right," as if to say, "Um-hmm, you're one of those." Then he said, "Well, how about I ask you a question?"

"Sure," I eagerly answered.

"Say there's a monk who lives in the Alps. Every day this monk walks three miles barefoot in the snow to a sacred site where he worships 'god.' He's near starvation, he's in bad health, yet every day for the rest of his life he makes the journey because he loves 'god.' One day he dies on his way back home in the snow."

Then the guy grinned at me. I knew what was coming. He asked, "Are you going to tell me that if this monk did not 'believe' in Jesus Christ, he went to hell?"

As I looked into his eyes with a lump in my throat, saddened by his question, I answered, "Bro, I'll let Jesus tell you in his own words: 'I am the way, and the truth, and the life; no one comes to the Father except through me' [John 14:6]. If the monk didn't believe in Jesus Christ as his Savior and through him alone receive forgiveness for his sins and life forever in heaven, the answer to your question—according to Jesus and Scripture—is yes, my friend, the monk is in hell."[1]

With controlled anger he responded, "I will never accept that! I will never believe that!"

To believe Jesus Christ is the one and only Savior and the only way to heaven is totally backward to our culture. To declare it and live it is costly. Jesus never promised popularity, promotions, or job security when we stand for his backward truth. He promised something far greater: himself, never leaving or forsaking us. If we are in a love relationship with the God who first loved us, then it doesn't matter that the world doesn't love us. Jesus warned,

> All the world will hate you because of me.
>
> Luke 21:17, my paraphrase

> If the world hates you, keep in mind that it hated me first. If you belonged to the world, it would love you as its own. As it is, you do not belong to the world, but I have chosen you out of the world. That is why the world hates you.
>
> John 15:18–19

The backward life is believing, declaring, living, standing—even dying for the truth that Jesus alone is Lord, God, and Savior.

What's the Deal?

The apostle Paul knew the "Jesus alone" truth was backward and costly. As recorded in Acts 16, Paul was beaten and thrown into prison after going to Macedonia to preach the gospel of the resurrection. In Acts 17, Paul traveled to Thessalonica to proclaim the gospel, and a mob attacked the home where he was staying. Paul then journeyed to Berea on the same mission, but the Thessalonians followed him and provoked the crowds to turn on him. Next we find Paul in the city of Athens, still declaring Jesus as the resurrected Lord.

Paul is alone, waiting for the others to join him, when he becomes "greatly distressed" at what he sees around him:

> While Paul was waiting for them in Athens, he was greatly distressed to see that the city was full of idols.
>
> Acts 17:16

Paul amazes me. He's been beaten, imprisoned, and run out of town for talking about Jesus. You would think he'd be pouting, throwing himself a pity party, saying, "God, what's the deal here? Am I really living in your will?" On the contrary, Paul doesn't focus on himself; he focuses on his mission. Sound backward? His urgent desire is to turn a wayward people to the God who will save them from a vain life, the God who will save them for an eternal life, the God who alone is worthy.

America 101

With mission in focus, a group of philosophers caught his eyes and ears. Paul was up for a good debate:

> A group of Epicurean and Stoic philosophers began to dispute with him. Some of them asked, "What is this babbler trying to say?"

Others remarked, "He seems to be advocating false gods." They said this because Paul was preaching the good news about Jesus and the resurrection.

Acts 17:18

Our Epicurean friends believed that pleasure and happiness at any cost was the life people were meant for. If they'd had a motto, it would have been "If it feels good, go for it!" Sound familiar? Think MTV.

Our Stoic pals believed *everything* was god. They believed some kind of "force" ruled the universe, one that was unable to love or care, neither evil nor good. Actually, they believed the universe *was* the force and inside each person was a "spark" of the force. The key to life, therefore, was to connect and become one with the "force." Can you say *Star Wars*—"May the force be with you"?

These guys thought Paul was an idiot. They thought he had picked up bits and pieces of various philosophies and fashioned them together to create his own truth. Although to them his resurrected Lord Jesus "theory" was foolish, they were still curious.

Then they took him and brought him to a meeting of the Areopagus [Mars Hill], where they said to him, "May we know what this new teaching is that you are presenting? You are bringing some strange ideas to our ears, and we want to know what they mean." (All the Athenians and the foreigners who lived there spent their time doing nothing but talking about and listening to the latest ideas.)

Acts 17:19–21

Some things never change. Today America spins its own wheels searching for and discussing the latest and greatest. The media feed it to us. The power of the media is off the stinkin' map. Millions of people are bombarded by television, the Internet, newspapers, magazines, and radio day in and day out. The media controls our culture and our people. Think about popular television talk shows, like the *Jerry Springer Show* among others. Think about all the "reality" shows.

Nothing is off-limits. Through the medium of media, every perverse subject under the sun is explored, revealed, or discussed, from bizarre sexual behavior to intense vulgar language to gory violence.

D. A. Carson, in his book *The Gagging of God*, hit the bull's-eye when he said, "The primary aim [of media] is to entertain, even shock, not think!"[2]

Don't get me wrong. I am not anti-media, or anti-entertainment. I am a movie addict. I have an iPod filled with every song I have ever loved since I was nine years old. My point is, however, that I believe we don't think through enough of what we are exposing ourselves and our families to. I am guilty of this. We may not be approaching entertainment, particularly some talk shows, radio shows, reality shows, and sitcoms (and yes, movies), with a critical or suspicious eye. The entertainment industry is constantly spending their time creating new ideas to shock and awe us. Many producers of all the above may have agendas to move us politically and spiritually, or to influence and desensitize us to destructive standards, morals, and values.

Fill-in-the-Blank Gods

Paul reveals a backward truth in application to this. He reveals the Christian approach. He didn't take a philosopher's latest and greatest ideas with a wink, a nod, and a smile. He critically thought through their religious approaches, arguments, and maybe even their motives. He didn't allow himself to be spoon fed the "latest ideas" without suspicion. And he did the unpopular thing—he stood his ground. He was not swayed. Though Paul had to deal with a bombardment of ideas, he did not succumb to or become controlled by them, like we often do with the media.

The religious ideas and philosophies seemed to be the entertainment of the day. Paul saw through their philosophies and wanted to declare backward truth. He confronted them by humbly positing his point of view. He met them on their turf and shared with them ultimate hope.

> Paul then stood up in the meeting of the Areopagus and said: "Men of Athens! I see that in every way you are very religious. For as I walked around and looked carefully at your objects of worship, I even found an altar with this inscription: TO AN UNKNOWN GOD. Now what you worship as something unknown I am going to proclaim to you."
>
> Acts 17:22–23

The culture of our day has its own version of an unknown god. I call it the "fill-in-the-blank god." This was best seen at the 2001 Citywide Prayer Service held at New York's Yankee stadium. When they prayed, America witnessed a "fill in the blank with your own god" buffet of religions.

Today's culture pressures Christ-followers to view Jesus as part of a "Heinz 57" variety of gods to worship: "You want to worship Buddha? Great! You want to worship Allah? Fabulous! You want to worship Buddha *and* Jesus? Go right ahead! What? You claim and worship *only* Jesus Christ as Lord and Savior? At the very least that's politically incorrect. At the very worst, it's a hate crime! You're an arrogant, dangerous religious Neanderthal." See, if you declare Jesus alone as Savior, the only one who must be worshiped as the true God, you will probably be branded an ignorant extremist and fundamentalist (and any other "ists" that are out there). We are so much like the Athenians.

Tough Love

During the days of the early church, Christ-followers would come to Rome proclaiming Jesus as Lord. At first, the idol-worshipers of Rome welcomed them. They invited the Christ-followers to the pantheon to put Jesus on display.

The pantheon was a temple that housed many different idol gods of the Roman culture. So the idol-worshipers escorted the Christ-followers into the pantheon and said, "Jesus? Cool! Okay, I'll tell you what: Let's move the moon goddess over this way, and put the sun god over here, and . . . there you go—it should be a nice fit for your Jesus right there."

Then the Christ-followers said, "Uh . . . no. I don't think you understand. Jesus is *the* Lord. Jesus is *the* Word. Jesus is *the* Son of God. Jesus is *the Savior.* He's not a statue. He's not another god from the religious assembly line or among the select few for the spiritual Hall of Fame. He *alone* is God."

That didn't sit well with the idol-worshipers. So the Christ-followers were mobbed, beaten, tossed into prison, or thrown to the lions.

True Christ-followers, then and now, must stand firm in the gospel of love. Backward-lifers cannot be provoked to violence—ever. No matter what is said or done, we must continue to stand and fight for the gospel in love—but a "tough love." We must stand strong in love. As backward as it is, love must rule the day. The apostle Paul said, "If I give all I possess to the poor and surrender my body to the flames, but have not love, I gain nothing" (1 Cor. 13:3). We must never forget this. We are to be compassionate, loving, and respectful of all people and religions. This does not mean "you have your truth, I have mine" tolerance. The truth must be made known in humility, love, and living a life worthy of the King we follow. Truth doesn't change despite the mood or movement. Jesus is Lord no matter what the circumstances. Jesus is the only Savior, no matter what Tom Cruise says.

The most backward and loving thing we can do for the world is to resolve to share the absolute truth that Jesus alone is Lord and Savior of all. God said through the apostle Peter,

> Salvation is found in no one else, for there is no other name under heaven given to men by which we must be saved.
>
> Acts 4:12

In 1999 I was director of high school ministries and associate teaching pastor at a church in Birmingham, Alabama. One Sunday, after I spoke to the adult congregation, the host mother of an exchange student from Thailand approached me. She shared that Joy, her exchange student, had "loved me to death" from the first moment she began attending our church. But now, the host mom said, she hated me.

Joy was a teenage Buddhist but considered herself a "Christian Buddhist." The previous Wednesday night, at our regular student outreach event, I spoke about how Jesus was the only way to God and the only way one could be saved. One of the points I made in my talk was that without embracing Jesus as one's Lord and Savior, a person is destined to spend eternity in a merciless, loveless hell separated from God forever. I also stated that Islam didn't save; Buddhism didn't save; New Ageism didn't save; works didn't save—only Jesus Christ could save. What Joy heard, according to her host mom, was that she was going to hell and all of her family who had already passed away (particularly the grandfather whom she adored) were in hell. Joy hated me for that.

My heart was broken—not because I had professed the backward truth of God but because I may have said it in a way that caused a broken relationship with Joy. As the host mom turned to leave, Joy walked by without even looking at me or speaking to me.

"Joy?" I said. "Can I talk to you for a sec?"

She stopped, head hanging down, eyes staring at the floor. Finally, she whispered a broken, "I . . . I guess."

I sat down next to Joy in the auditorium, away from the crowds. I lowered my head as far as I could to try to look into her eyes. After getting her to look at me, I said, "Joy, I love you. And I know you really don't like me right now. I think you might even hate me for some of the things I preached the other night."

Looking down to avoid my eyes, she just nodded her head up and down.

With tears filling my eyes, I continued, "Joy, I want you to know first and foremost that I love you and it is absolutely ripping my heart out knowing that you don't like me anymore. God loves you so, so much." Then, fumbling for words, I said, "Joy, can I say a couple of things about what I talked about the other night at Student Outreach? First of all, I want you to know that if I came across as arrogant or prideful with my words, I am so sorry. Please forgive me. I was dead wrong."

She briefly looked up at me with tears rolling down her cheeks, nodded her head up and down, and then dropped her head again.

"But . . ." I cautioned, "Joy, please listen and understand. *What* I said, and not how I said it, is the absolute truth. Jesus truly is the only way to heaven, the only way to God. And for that truth, Joy, I cannot apologize. It is the perfect truth of God."

I paused for a moment, hoping she would respond. Still she stared at the ground with tears falling into her lap.

"Joy, the most loving thing I could possibly say to you or do for you is to lead you to the absolute truth that Jesus Christ is God's Son and the only Savior of the world. I will never quit talking about that on Wednesday nights, Sunday mornings, or when I'm hanging out with people. This doesn't mean I don't love you. This doesn't mean that you are not welcome because of what you believe. It just means that I will never lie to you or compromise this truth with you: Jesus truly is the only way to heaven."

Finally Joy opened up. "I just don't understand. Buddhism doesn't teach that. What about my grandfather? He wasn't a Christian." By now Joy was sobbing.

I let her cry for a moment while I sat in silence. Actually, I was praying about what in the world to say without compromising the truth. Then I answered, "Joy, my heart breaks for your grandfather. My heart also breaks for my family and friends who have died without believing in Jesus as their Lord and Savior. That's why I am so passionate about telling you and everybody else the absolute truth. I don't want that to happen to anybody else I know and love.

As far as our family and friends who have never believed, well, let's not focus on that. It's between them and God now."

Joy wasn't giving an inch. After a few minutes of awkward silence, she said she needed to go.

I mentioned to her that I would apologize to the entire audience at the upcoming Student Outreach for perhaps coming across as prideful, uncaring, or arrogant in speaking about these hard truths. And I did just that, but I also followed up by saying that I could not apologize for God's backward truth—that Jesus is the only way, truth, and life and no one goes to the Father but through him (see John 14:6). Amazingly, at the end of the service, Joy thanked me for the apology.

I thought for sure that I wouldn't be seeing much of Joy around the church anymore. But she kept coming, even more faithfully than the church kids. What I didn't know was that a group of about four Christian teenage girls from the high school ministry had taken Joy under their wings. They invited Joy to the mall and painted their nails together; they did everything together. Spiritual matters would come up casually between the girls and Joy. The girls boldly shared the backward truth of Jesus. All the while they marinated Joy with love.

About six months later, Joy walked up to me with a gargantuan smile.

She said, "Jarrod, I am a Christian!"

"What?" I barked.

She giggled herself into an all-out laugh and announced, *"I am a Christian!"* With my mouth hanging open, I stared at her like she'd just won the lottery. Then I hugged her as hard as I could.

A few weeks later I took Joy for ice cream. "Joy, do you understand that you can't be a Buddhist Christian, and that salvation can only be through Christ alone?" I asked.

"Oh yeah," she said matter-of-factly while licking her ice cream.

"Joy, that means you are renouncing Buddhism for Jesus alone. Does that make sense?"

She looked up at me with a big smile and a gleam in her eye and said, "Jarrod, I renounce Buddhism. I love Jesus!"

Give Me the Gospel or Give Me Death

God's backward truth makes an impact. It made an impact on a young guy from Bardstown Road in Louisville, and it made an impact on a teenage Buddhist from Thailand. We aren't responsible for the impact. We are responsible for the backward truth. The impact is up to God.

We are also to be responsible *with* the backward truth—living it, sharing it, defending it, standing for it, and if need be, dying for it. If you are still an unbeliever and feel chafed by all that you have read, especially in this chapter (and if you made it this far, by the way, thank you for reading this book!), would you think about something? If you possessed what you knew to be the absolute, soul-saving, life-changing truth that the whole world needed in order to live abundantly now and for eternity, what would you do? Would you not live it? Would you not declare it? Would you not defend it? Would you not die for it?

Sadly, some profess they are Christians yet do none of the above. They may declare Jesus as Lord, but they do it with anger, hostility, and threats against those who disagree or mock them. Plain and simple, they aren't the real thing, or at best they're extremely misguided. Instead of dwelling on Christians who seem hypocritical, search out the backward-lifers. They are the true Christ-followers.

Those four teenage girls who stood for truth and loved Joy into Christianity are the backward life in motion. They didn't dwell on their differences of beliefs or culture, nor their fears or concerns that they might say something offensive. They embraced Joy—relationally and spiritually. Now that smiling, giddy, joyful young woman is in Thailand standing for the backward truth, living the backward life. The impact of the backward life knows no bounds.

13

The Backward Mind

"Free your mind . . ."

Morpheus to Neo
in *The Matrix*

In the Saturday, April 1, 2000, edition of the *Birmingham News*, I discovered a weird article about a headless chicken. The article stated:

> For 18 months in the 1940s, it seemed as if Mike the headless chicken might be immortal.
>
> The rooster belonged to Fruita farmer Lloyd Olsen, who planned to put Mike into the cooking pot and lopped off his head at the base of the skull to leave as much of the tasty neck as possible.
>
> But Mike just fluffed up his feathers—although he could only go through the motions of pecking for food, and when he tried to crow, a gurgle came out. But he was still alive the next morning. Olsen started putting feed and water directly into Mike's gullet with an eyedropper.

When Mike was still alive a week later, Olsen took him to University of Utah scientists, who theorized Mike had enough of a brain stem left to live headless. He made it into *Life* magazine and the *Guinness Book of World Records* and was a popular attraction until he choked to death on a corn kernel in an Arizona motel.[1]

I would have retired my farming shoes forever. Can you imagine seeing a rooster walking around, going through the motions of being a chicken for over a year—without a head?

Perhaps it's less astonishing, but it's true: there are Christians going through the motions, giving their heads away to things of this world day after day, year after year. Many of us who confess Jesus as our Lord and Savior run around like rooster Mike with our heads cut off, putting our minds on a plate of immoral, violent, and thoughtless entertainment. This should be troubling to us, but it's not.

Headless Christians are running around with no eyes to see God, no ears to hear God, no lips to praise God, and ultimately no passion for God because we have given our minds over to the things of this world. We don't seem to act, think, or feel any differently than the world. No one can find any difference between the pursuits of the world and the pursuits of Christians. We get a kernel of God at church or a retreat, camp, or conference. Instead of feeding on it as life-giving nourishment, we often choke on it because it clashes with where our minds have been the days, hours, or minutes before.

We need new minds.

A new mind is a backward mind that goes against the current. It's a mind of discernment between the things of this world and the things of God. It's a mind set apart for God.

Body for Life

Therefore, I urge you, brothers, in view of God's mercy, to offer your bodies as living sacrifices, holy and pleasing to God—this is your [reasonable or] spiritual act of worship.

Romans 12:1

Paul prefaces his instruction about the mind with preparation of the body. He pleads with us first to give our bodies to God. Why? Our bodies are made by God and for God. How are we to offer God our bodies? *As living sacrifices, holy and pleasing to him.*

When Paul says to offer your body to God, he is using the same word that was used for the sacrifices God directed the people of Israel to make. Priests offered as sacrifices animals butchered on an altar, blood flowing down, set on fire, smoke rising up as incense to God. Paul says that God expects us to offer our bodies not as suicide bombers but as living sacrifices. With every day and every breath, we lay our bodies on the altar before God and say, "I am yours, God. No matter what it costs me, Lord, my body is yours." What does this actually look like in our everyday lives?

Guys, maybe it's when you sit down in front of your computer to check your email. You notice there's a message with an attachment from "Desperate Debbie" with the subject line "X X X: Click here!" In that moment, your heart beats, your palms sweat, you're about to tap the "click here." But you close your eyes and pray, "O Lord, everything in me wants to check this out. I pray, Holy Spirit, for your help. Lord, my eyes are only for you." Then, by faith, you take the mouse, move your cursor, and click "delete." After that, you go to your delete file and click "delete" again. Your eyes have become a living sacrifice to God.

It's when you turn on the radio or put in the CD to listen to music that tells you to go smoke something, drink something, have sex with somebody, curse somebody, fight somebody, or kill somebody, and then you pray, "Lord, I like the beat. I like the song. Everything within me wants to listen. Help me, Lord. By faith, I'm not going to listen. Jesus, my ears are only for you." Then, you change stations or perhaps turn off the radio, or toss the CD in the trash as a "sacrifice." Your ears are a living sacrifice to God.

Maybe you're hanging out with friends at the coffee shop and you have some juicy dirt on someone, or a dirty joke, that if shared will make you the flavor of the moment. Yet instead of gossiping, lying, or telling a joke that cheapens you and breaks God's heart, you pray, "Lord God, I confess I want the attention. I want the laughter. I want the popularity. Help me, Lord, to obey you. Jesus, my lips are for you alone." Then, by faith, you bite your tongue or perhaps walk away. In that moment your lips have become a living sacrifice to God.

As a living sacrifice you act by faith. Through the power of the Holy Spirit, your mind moves your will to take action by faith. When you are tempted to give your eyes, ears, or lips away to things of this world, it's your faith-soaked mind (a backward mind) that clings to the fact that God himself is the fullness of joy and the pleasure of your existence. Sure, those worldly things may satisfy for a moment, a weekend, or a year, but Jesus Christ is the One who satisfies every craving of your soul forever. You see, eternal life is not just the length of life but the quality of life—a life fully satisfied in Jesus.

This living sacrifice is "holy and pleasing to God." *Holy* means "set apart, pure, without any stain or blemish." God wants our eyes set apart, our ears set apart, our mouths set apart, our everything set apart, all for him and his glory. Why? We're made for him.

In the big picture, salvation in Jesus makes you cleaner than Cascade. Nonetheless, we dirty up our lives every day, offering our minds and bodies to worldly pleasures that aren't pleasing to God. When that happens, we must confess to God—which means to agree with God—that we looked at porn, listened to a degrading song, gossiped about a girl out of jealousy, told a dirty joke, or lied, and we sinned against him. Renouncing those actions or thoughts, we must turn from doing them and run back to Jesus.

The World's Molding Wheel

Do not conform any longer to the pattern of this world, but be transformed by the renewing of your mind. Then you will be able to test and approve what God's will is—his good, pleasing and perfect will.

Romans 12:2

Now Paul is getting to the crux of the problem. Basically, it's the spiritual side of the Avril Lavigne song "Complicated."

> You know you're not fooling anyone when you have become
> Somebody else round everyone else. . . .
> Trying to be cool you look like a fool to me.

Paul begs for us to no longer be conformed to the pattern of the world. Conforming to the pattern of the world is what Avril Lavigne described in her song, though we'll interpret it spiritually. It's acting differently from the reality of what God has done within us. We try to be someone else around everyone else instead of becoming more like Jesus by connecting deeply to the grace given to us by God and the Spirit of God within us. Instead of being backward to the world, we're running in the pattern of the world—away from God and against God.

I picked up an issue of *Rolling Stone* a while back following the Video Music Awards on MTV. I'm not picking on Avril Lavigne (because the world is full of lots of examples), but God used a photograph to reveal a piercing truth to me. Inside the magazine was a picture of Kelly Osbourne and Avril Lavigne glaring into the camera with scowls on their faces and their middle fingers at full mass.

Right there, I thought, *is a portrait of the pattern of this world.*

Disturbing, isn't it? Giving our minds and bodies over to the ways of the world is like holding hands with a world that is flipping God off. That's tough to swallow. But sin is no joke. As a believer, I am heartbroken to think that I would give my mind and body over to that kind of conformity.

In my last year of junior college, I had to take an elective class of some sort. I didn't want to waste my time on a bogus class like physics, law, or political science. So I tackled Ceramic Pottery Making 101. Picture me, a tall, goofy, bull-in-a-china-shop guy, with a bunch of little grandmas who took the class as a hobby and an angelic teacher.

I was determined to impress my fifteen grandmas by becoming the best pottery maker that semester. Just to set the bar of expectations, so to speak, I sat down on this little stool, found the pedal to a weird-looking machine, and began pumping that pedal until I had the machine buzzing like a fan. The teacher walked over, no doubt to praise my commanding performance. Instead, she put her hand on my shoulder and said, "Son, the sewing machine is for the sewing class; the ceramics class meets over here."

Okay, I wasn't that clueless, but I was pretty close. All semester we took turns on the pottery-making thingy, pushing the pedal, spinning the wheel, and putting our hands around wet clay to form it into, hopefully, what we had envisioned. Halfway through the semester, my new grandmas had made vases, baskets, cups, bowls, and crosses. All I had to show was a ceramic bowl. It looked like a canoe. Even today, more than a decade later, my mom proudly displays my work in the attic.

You and I are like clay. There are fingers working to conform us to an image. We are on the pottery wheel of life, continually being molded and shaped by something. Whose fingers are doing the molding—the world's or Jesus'?

Free Your Mind

Paul, thank goodness, didn't leave us hanging. He went from "conformed" to transformed: "Do not conform any longer to the pattern of this world, but be transformed" (Rom. 12:2). Transforming is a process by which our behavior and actions are being continually changed from the way they are now to the behavior and actions of the Holy Spirit within us—love, joy, peace, patience, kindness, goodness, faithfulness, gentleness, and self-control (Gal. 5:22–23).

You might remember from a science lesson in your junior high days that the word for *transformed* comes from *metamorphosis*. Think of a caterpillar becoming a butterfly. When you become a believer, you are in the process of breaking out of the cocoon of self and sin and transforming into who you are in Jesus.

The world is so seductive, though, with its barrage of instant gratification and self-motivation. So how do we stay free from its grip? How do we get out of the cocoon of self and sin? "By the renewing of your mind" (Rom. 12:2).

Morpheus said to Neo in *The Matrix*, "Free your mind," and we nodded and said, "Cool!" Yet for the past nearly two thousand years Paul has said, "Free your mind by renewing it," and we've yawned. What does Paul mean when he tells us to renew our minds? He's saying that an *Extreme Makeover* episode is needed for our minds. He's saying, "Renovate your mind."

Seeking God through Scripture and prayer brings Jesus through the door of our dilapidated minds, where he says, "Let's take out these walls of selfishness, worldly desires, dirty thoughts and language, and disobedience. Now build walls of faith, holiness, purity, and obedience. And what is that hideous attitude doing there? Get that outta here, and let's hang my attitude of humility and love there instead. Whoa, this pornographic wallpaper—tear it down and paint the walls with my glory. Wow, even the framing is rotted by guilt, shame, regret, fear, anger, and anxiety. Let's start from scratch and erect steel beams of grace, freedom, forgiveness, and joy. This mind is going to be my home."

Like renovating a house, creating a renovated mind doesn't happen overnight. Sin and self keep returning in ravenous termite form to destroy all that God is doing in your mind. It takes time, work, and energy for your mind to be renovated: time seeking God through his Word and prayer; work at turning away from self-destruction and turning to God for the glory of his kingdom; energy, fueled by God's grace, to obey him when temptation pounds on the door of your mind.

The mind is like a computer hard drive of the heart. Whatever enters the mind automatically downloads into the heart and ultimately surfaces through our attitudes, language, behavior, and relationships.

If you expose your mind to entertainment that glorifies unmarried sex, nudity, adultery, homosexuality, violence, and bad language, then you allow into your mind "soul viruses" that will infect your heart. This hinders the renewing of your mind in the pursuit of God.

Renewing your mind comes from "reading, pleading, and bleeding." Let me explain each one.

Reading

The Bible contains the mind of God relevant to every aspect of life. Scripture is God-breathed. It is the mind of God, revealing his heart and his ways. The Word of God woos us toward his love and warns us of his wrath; it is the fire, the hammer, and the sword of God to daily renovate our minds.

"Is not my word like fire?" declares the LORD, "and like a hammer which shatters a rock?"

Jeremiah 23:29 NASB

For the word of God is living and active. Sharper than any double-edged sword, it penetrates even to dividing soul and spirit, joints and marrow; it judges the thoughts and attitudes of the heart.

Hebrews 4:12

Read the Word of God slowly. Meditate on it. The truth of God's Word breaks the hardness of our hearts and our minds. We become desensitized and misled by our culture, trapped by bad habits, and cut deeply by life. We can become scarred by disturbing images we have seen, harsh words that have been spoken, and memories of our past. The Word of God heals wounds, soothes scars, brings freedom from the traps. It takes the light of God's truth in your mind to expose the lies and deceptions that are lurking within cultural and religious movements, beliefs, and values. Feelings are a battle also. When our feelings and thoughts say one thing about us, God, or others, God's Word is the anchor of truth. The Word of God gives us the true, yet backward, worldview.

Pleading

Prayer is not something you do at church or before meals. Prayer is the groaning of your heart and the breath of your soul. It flows from an ever-increasing awareness of Christ's presence within you. Go to the book of Psalms in Scripture for clear evidence of David's pleading heart. Prayer is not just boxed into quiet times or crisis times either. It is a steady conversation with God at all times.

> And pray in the Spirit on all occasions with all kinds of prayers and requests.
>
> Ephesians 6:18

> Pray continually.
>
> 1 Thessalonians 5:17

Whether you are in the shower, on the treadmill, in the car, checking email, listening to your iPod, watching the game, or standing in line at the mall, prayer is the continuous intimate conversation with God that brings you heartbeat to heartbeat with him. Prayer reveals sin and brings us to repentance. Prayer guards the mind against temptation. It reveals greater knowledge of our Lord Jesus Christ.

Bleeding

Bleeding means laying all of you—heart, mind, body, soul, dreams, self-esteem, ambitions, plans, relationships, future—on the altar every day as a living sacrifice to God. It's an obedient life that seeks to be holy and pleasing to God no matter the cost. It's a backward life that seeks to glorify God in all things, laying down our own plans and dreams and replacing them with his.

So whether you eat or drink or whatever you do, do it all for the glory of God.

1 Corinthians 10:31

Drinking Dr Pepper, eating extra-hot buffalo wings, downloading on iTunes, and even talking on a cell phone can become spiritual acts of worship. The world calls that fanatical; God calls it worship. The world calls it weird; Paul calls it a renovated—backward—mind.

God's Will for Your Life

The splendor of having a backward mind is we're spared from feeling that we are at the mercy of chance, luck, or circumstances. We don't have to go through life wondering and wandering. If we are seeking God first, we can be confident that we are in God's will, no matter what's happening in our lives. We don't have to fret over where to go to school, what career to pursue, where to settle down, or who to marry. We'll discover that God has us in his good, perfect, loving will.

Seek first the kingdom of God and His righteousness, and all these things shall be added to you.

Matthew 6:33 NKJV

Frank

Several years ago I was on a mission project in Philadelphia. We were walking along Kensington Avenue passing out Slim Jims and vanilla cookies to the homeless. Kensington Avenue was known at the time as the crack capital of the world. From the look of things, I believed it. Prostitutes, crack addicts, and little blue-green crack baggies lined the street in the early morning hours.

One night I met a middle-aged homeless man named Frank. After a few minutes of awkward conversation, he finally opened up.

He told me that he was hooked on crack and had lost everything. Just two years earlier he had been married with two daughters, a business owner, and a part-time minister. The downward spiral began when he reached a point of burnout, felt sorry for himself, and isolated himself from family and friends. He filled his time and mind with worldly pleasures that gave him brief but fleeting release.

He said he found himself riding around alone some nights drinking a beer. Soon that beer became a six-pack. Then the six-pack became a pint of hard liquor. Then one night he walked into the bathroom of a bar and discovered one of those little blue-green baggies containing a crack rock. He quickly tucked it into his pocket, drove out of town, and smoked it under a bridge. His words to me were, "Man, I was hooked for life. I've lost everything. I can't quit. It's impossible to quit."

I tried talking to him about the forgiveness, love, and freedom found in Jesus. He acted as if I was the millionth person who had shared this with him. Maybe I was. In any case, he wasn't interested. He did allow me to pray with him, and afterward I asked, "Frank, can you tell me how to guard myself and others from this ever happening to us?"

"Yeah, man," he said. "It's the little things. All you hear about today are the big things: don't drink, don't do drugs, don't have sex until you get married. Those are cool things, but there's a lot more to it. It's the little things that get you. What you watch on television, what movies you see, what music you listen to, what magazines you look at and read, what you dwell on, what you talk about. That's what creeps in and gets you."

Then Frank gave me an illustration I will never forget, one that I share every time I talk about having a pure mind. "Take a gigantic, five-hundred-year-old tree," he said, "the biggest, most beautiful tree you have ever seen. All it takes is one little beetle. One little beetle gets into that tree and kills it. That's how it is with those little things, man. They creep in and mess you up."

I was deeply convicted. And I asked myself the question that I want to ask you: What beetles have you allowed into your life and mind?

Self-pity?

Anger?

Bitterness?

Immoral TV programs?

Movies filled with sex and violence?

Violent video games?

Music with a great beat but lyrics about sex, violence, drug and alcohol abuse, and the degradation of women?

What are the beetles? Where are they?

Beetles are absolutely hideous! What would you do if you felt one crawling up your neck and into your ear? You would scream, kick, swipe, and whatever else it took to get that little monster off of you. Then, when it hit the floor, *STOMP*!

That's the passion we need to rid ourselves of the "beetles" of sin. Not too long ago I met a young guy, probably in his early twenties, who confessed to me that he was addicted to Internet porn. He just couldn't stop himself, he said.

I asked him, "How serious are you about getting rid of this thing? Try this. Put your computer in the living room, dining room, or wherever, as long as it is in a public place, so whenever you are on the computer your family can see what you are viewing. Make a commitment not to check email or go online unless someone is home. Have a friend put a block on your computer."

"I've already tried the porn block," he said, "but I can get past it every time."

"Okay then," I responded, "you have to put it in a public room and confide in a friend who will be tough and hold you accountable not to view the stuff. If that doesn't work, get rid of your computer."

He just glared at me.

So I asked him again, "What are you willing to do to conquer this, bro? How serious are you?"

What about you? Can I ask you again: What beetles are in your life? And how serious are you about conquering them?

A backward mind is impossible without Jesus, through his Holy Spirit, renovating and enthroning your mind through reading (Scripture), pleading (prayer), and bleeding (obedience). The result is a new mind that desires to honor him, with a banner above your mind's door that says, "Whatever is true, whatever is noble, whatever is right, whatever is pure, whatever is lovely, whatever is admirable—if anything is excellent or praiseworthy—think about such things" (Phil. 4:8).

Sound backward?

I once had Philippians 4:8 written on typing paper and taped to the glass of my television set. It began as a great tool to challenge and encourage me to guard my mind. But after about a week, I was flipping the typing paper over the top of the television without giving it a second thought, indulging in TV shows that didn't honor God. The point is this: Philippians 4:8 has to be more than an inspiration or an aspiration. It must be actively pursued, daily, hourly, minute-by-minute.

How serious are you about having a backward mind? A mind conformed to the world leads to living a Christian life that goes through the motions with no eyes, ears, or lips for God.

Just as Mike the headless chicken went through the motions of pecking and crowing like a chicken, so too can we be headless Christians going through the motions of Christianity. Don't be like Mike.

14

The Backward Faith

"Sweeeeeeet Emoooootion . . ."

Aerosmith

One year I spoke at a winter youth retreat in Indiana. A couple of months later I checked my email one morning to discover a message from a teenage girl who had attended the retreat. Her email sounded desperate. She was crying out to me for a lifeline. Below is the email she sent me, word for word. See if you relate to what she wrote:

Jarrod,
Hello. I want you to pray for me because my relationship with God isn't the same anymore! After the Winter Retreat, God and I were awesome. . . . My life revolved around God and not the world! But now all of the sudden I have went down . . . praying isn't the same! I can't force myself to do it anymore!

It's boring and I don't know why it's boring . . . something has happened! The feeling has faded! I know that a relationship with

God isn't a feeling ... but I can't do it without the feeling! I need
something, and youth group isn't doing it for me! I need something
really spiritual and that isn't till Ichthus [a Christian Woodstock]
and that [isn't until] April. . . . I am scared of what will happen until
then. The world is a scary place without God and right now . . . he's
not there and I am trying . . . but it's not coming! Please give me
some advice! Thank you, Jarrod!

"The *feeling* has faded. I can't do it without the *feeling*!" Did she
take the words right out of your mouth? Sure, she's a teenage girl,
but this isn't just a teenage thing any more than it's just a girl thing.
It's a "one size fits all" thing. This is a universal issue faced by all
Christians. I once found myself falling victim to the very same thing.
I know godly grannies with the same struggles. Let's get real here.
If we Christ-followers lack those sweet emotions—the feelings, the
God-bumps, the God-tingles, the warm fuzzies—then we think
there is something wrong with us or something wrong with God.
We fall victim to self once again.

Many Christ-followers live from conference to conference, from
women's retreat to women's retreat, from mission trip to mission
trip, from beach camp to beach camp, to get a spiritual feelings fix
so they'll feel like reading their Bible, so they'll feel like praying, so
they'll feel like putting others first, so they'll *not* feel like holding
a grudge, so they'll *not* feel like watching porn, and so they'll *not*
feel like partying.

For many Christians, feelings make their spiritual world go 'round.
And why not? Feelings are normal, right? Well, to some extent, but
more about that later. The bigger picture is this: the feelings addic-
tion dominates our culture and bleeds into our walk with Jesus. A
while back I saw a Coke commercial with a young man and woman
in an empty theater watching an old movie. They turn to each other
with goo-goo eyes, and the next thing you know they're dancing
in the aisles. The scene cuts to two dancing Coca-Cola cans with a
logo that invites us to "Do What Feels Good."

Feelings can rule our lives, including mine at times. A few years ago, if there had been a twelve-step program for this, I'd have been the first to stand up and say, "Hi. My name is Jarrod, and I'm an emotionaholic." I love sweet emotions. I love feelings. I always have. When I was a young Christian, the only time I thought I was saved was when I felt God. The only time I obeyed God with joy was when tears puddled in my eyes at the mention of John 3:16. If I didn't feel God, if I wasn't moved to tears with thoughts of God, then my "self" ruled, and I went wherever my feelings took me—anger, bitterness, moodiness, cursing, sexual fantasies. What about you?

Our backward God says faith rules, not feelings. Paul didn't say, "We walk by feelings, not by faith." He said, "We live by faith, not by sight" (2 Cor. 5:7). The feeling world lives for what it sees. The backward life lives by the reality of what is hoped for, the certainty of what is not seen and not always felt. It's radically backward not to live according to what we see and what we feel.

The backward life calls for a passionate faith. Faith demands passion. Please understand, I am not talking about passion in terms of "feeling on fire for God." I am talking about a passion that perseveres when the feelings aren't there. The backward life is not a faith fueled by passion but a passion fueled by faith—a backward passion. Soak that in for a moment.

Don't get me wrong; feelings of passion must flow from our faith at times. If this never happened, we would need to examine our hearts. The reality still remains that feelings of passionate faith aren't always there. The kind of passion revealed and called for in this chapter is a backward passion—the kind of passion that's set in the concrete of faith, not built in the sand of feelings.

The author of Hebrews reminds us,

And without faith it is impossible to please God, because anyone who comes to him must believe that he exists and that he rewards those who earnestly seek him.

Hebrews 11:6

Notice he didn't say, "without feelings it is impossible to please God," but "without faith it is impossible to please God." Faith pleases God, not feelings of passion. What freedom! I don't have to feel guilty when my spiritual "sweet emotion" is not there.

Thinking that as Christians we must have feelings of passion for God 24/7 can be as overwhelming as thinking we must push our cars every day instead of driving them. Why do we exhaust ourselves pushing these feelings of passion, when faith is the very vehicle that carries us?

Did you catch that word *earnestly* at the end of Hebrews 11:6? Sounds like a word of passion, doesn't it? Earnest faith equals passionate faith.

So what is passion? Passion is pursuing the goal, even when you don't *feel* like it, even when it hurts, even when it costs you.

Lance Armstrong won his seventh consecutive Tour de France bike race in 2005, breaking the world record. This is a man who has been fighting cancer for years. Do you think he always felt like climbing on his bike every day, riding hundreds of miles to train for the race, while fighting the sickening effects of chemotherapy? No. But he did it even when he didn't feel like it, despite the risk to his health or his life. He didn't let his pain or his feelings stop him. That's passion.

During the race in 2003, Armstrong rounded a curve when the handlebars of his bike snagged the purse of a woman who had leaned out of the crowd while clapping and cheering him on. Armstrong nose-dived onto the pavement. He got up, wiped off the dirt, sweat, and blood, and climbed right back on his bike. He rode on to the finish line, winning the toughest bike race in the world. Do you think Armstrong felt like getting up off the pavement and climbing back onto his bike to complete the race? No way. But he pursued the goal even when he didn't feel like it, even when it hurt. That's passion.

How about Ben Comen? I learned about Ben Comen in an October 13, 2003, *Sports Illustrated* article by Rick Reilly. Ben Comen

runs races but will never win. Ben has cerebral palsy. According to
Reilly, while the winner of a 3.1 mile race finishes in 16 minutes, it
takes Ben 51 minutes. Ben's disease "seizes his muscles and contorts
his body and gives him the balance of a Times Square drunk," says
Reilly. Regardless, Ben faithfully competes in all his high school
marathons.[1]

Reilly asks us to consider what Ben faces with every race,
which would be more than enough to make you and me quit. He
writes,

> Imagine what it feels like to . . . [never] beat anybody to the finish
> line. Imagine dragging along that stubborn left side, pulling that
> unbending iron of a leg around to the front and pogo-sticking off
> it to get back to his right. Worse, he lifts his feet so little that he
> trips on anything—a twinkie sized rock, a licorice-thick branch, the
> cracks between linoleum tiles. Worst, he falls hard. His brain can't
> send signals fast enough for his arms to cushion his fall, so he often
> smacks his head or his face or his shoulder.[2]

Reilly mentions the time Ben was making his final approach and
fell within ten yards of the finish line: "Ben went through a 15-second
process of getting his bloody knees under him, his balance back, and
his forward motion going again—and he finished."

Ben finishes every race, but always bloody and bruised. "Oh, he
always loses—Ben barely finishes ahead of the sunset, forget other
runners. But he hasn't quit once. Through rain, wind or welt, he
always crosses the finish line," states Reilly.[3]

Ben punishes his body, yet he will never, ever, ever win a race.
Does he seem stubborn? Does he seem foolish? Or does Ben seem
passionate? Do you really think Ben feels like running in every race,
knowing that he'll finish bloody and bruised? Do you think he looks
forward to falling on his face when he trips over his own feet? Is it
conceivable to think that Ben delights in the possibility that if he
falls the wrong way, it could cost him his life? No. Ben pursues the
goal, no matter what. That's passion.

Most people would have thrown in the towel facing the obstacles that Lance and Ben have faced. Lance and Ben don't fit the mold. They're backward.

Some Christians throw in the towel when things get tough. "As long as Christianity brings security, happiness, comfort, and a pain-free existence, then praise Jesus," they say. But the minute the feelings fade, the painful obstacles of life enter, and worldly security and happiness go "poof," then it's back to looking out for number one again. This isn't faith that pleases God. These are religious charades that sicken God. Only one kind of faith pleases God: the passionate faith that perseveres. It's countercultural. It's backward.

Like Lance and Ben, another man was backward to the world. And it wasn't his physical prowess that set him apart; it was his backward passion for Jesus. Talk about a passionate faith—none can compare to Paul.

When he wrote the book of Philippians, Paul was writing a letter from prison. Not a letter from a hotel room at the latest Christian conference but from *prison*—a prison that was cold, dark, and lonely. And he was chained to a prison guard. Ponder that for a moment. If Paul wanted to cry in despair, the guard was there. If Paul wanted to privately pour out his heart to God in anger or despair, the guard was there. If Paul needed to go to the toilet, the guard was still there.

Throughout life we face our own dark, cold prisons of sorrow, despair, and loneliness. We can feel as if God is far away and we are completely alone. We can feel hopelessly chained to the bully of depression, bitterness, doubt, or anger. No matter how much we drown ourselves in eBay, no matter how much we tell ourselves "this too shall pass," and no matter how often we pencil on a smile—the bully is always there. It can be enough to make you want to take your ball and go home. It can be enough to make you want to quit life and faith altogether. How do I know? Let's just say I've had my own bully.

I just recently discovered the identity of my own bully. I knew the chains were there since college. I knew there was something attached to the other end of those chains. Sometimes it was like a best friend, swinging the chains like an exciting game of jump rope; other times it was like the Grim Reaper, wrapping the chains around my neck, choking the life out of me.

I was a youth pastor when someone pointed out this bully in my life and gave it a nickname. I had a yearly evaluation by the executive director of student ministries at the church where I was serving. "Excellence and growth in every area; not one negative mark for anything," was the summary of the evaluation as I recall (you don't really think I'd remember anything bad, do you?). "But . . ." she said.

Uh-oh. *But?* I thought as my eyes got big and I squeezed the sides of the chair.

"Jarrod, there is one thing. About every three months you seem to go through a 'gunk.' You're not the same person. You isolate yourself. You don't talk to anybody. It puts the staff on edge. We don't know what is wrong with you. We don't know what to say to you or how to talk to you."

Ahh, the "gunk." I recalled the fires that raged in my head, the sadness that reigned in my heart during those times. But I had no idea what it was. I had no clue how I was coming across to others. I felt ashamed. "The gunk." I was almost relieved it had a name now, although I had considered it something everyone had.

Fast-forward to my three and a half years of seminary. I lived in an eleven-by-fourteen room. I intentionally isolated myself from any meaningful, lasting relationships (which I painfully regret), with the idiotic excuse that I was there to learn and not to make friends. The bully on the end of the chain got stronger, dragging me around like Frodo and Sam first did with Gollum in the Lord of the Rings. Sleepless nights increased. Fortunately, I journaled a lot during those years, and it later helped me.

Fast-forward again, now to my marriage. Within a couple of months, my wife, Christie, knew something wasn't right about me. One minute I would be spewing out superhuman amounts of work, rambling on and on about things that didn't make sense, and popping off strange ideas as fast as a lit pack of Black Cat firecrackers; the next minute I would have this raging anger inside with no explanation. Then a day or a week or two later, I would be in utter despair, crying uncontrollably, feeling as if my guts were turning inside out and my mind was literally on fire. I couldn't sleep. My stomach ached almost every day. I couldn't find pleasure in anything. And the guilt, oh, the guilt! I was speaking at a young adult gathering called Area One every week as well as traveling and speaking about the good news of Jesus all over the country. In the eyes of many, I was a spiritual hero. But I was falling apart at the seams. I thought the guilt would ultimately do me in.

These patterns went from being the exception, happening once every three months or so, to controlling my life month after month. Christie, being a school counselor, detected something. She had never seen it in me before because our entire dating life and engagement were long-distance. She and I looked through my journals and were shocked by the discovery. Eighty percent of my journals revealed suicidal thoughts, raging anger, outrageous and embarrassing ideas, and the fear of abandonment by God—then pleading with God not to let me go and vowing to God that I would never let him go. By God's grace, in the midst of this anguish, faith held fast. Eventually, Christie took a day off from work, and together we visited a psychiatrist. A counselor and two doctors later, diagnosis: bipolar disorder type 2 (manic depression).

Besides feeling like a freak, I thanked God that I finally had a name for this very real bully. Since then, God has provided the medical help and professional and relational support that I needed. Even more importantly, he has made it clearer than ever before that he was as near to me then—no matter how manic or depressed I was—as he is to me now. I can't tell you enough about the freedom that has flooded my soul anew: the freedom of knowing that God is near and God is good. Feelings don't please God; faith does.

Giving in to the mania and depression and blaming God for "the way he made me" would have been a typical response. But by God's grace I know that I'm not typical but backward. I wrapped my arms around Jesus, dug my nails into his back, and held on to him. And God held on to me. He still does.

There's only one way to break the chains and fight our bullies: the backward passion of faith. Not for the sake of just being free but for the sake of knowing and following Jesus, displaying to the world that he alone is worthy of passionate faith, no matter what our chains or bullies.

With all that the apostle Paul is facing, you'd expect him to fall apart at the seams. But Paul isn't typical either; he's backward. In that dark, cold, lonely prison, chained to a Roman guard, Paul says, "I rejoice" (Phil. 1:18). Paul witnesses to others through his letters. He writes, "Rejoice in the Lord" (Phil. 3:1). Feelings do not produce this kind of joy. Paul's faith in God produces that joy. It pours out as encouragement and inspiration to others—all from the inside of a prison cell.

The backward life is a life in which no matter what our circumstances, through passionate faith, we rejoice in God and refuse feelings of self-pity, moving others to find their joy in God as well. The backward life reaches out for God and others not just when we feel like it, not just when it's convenient, but especially when everything is against us.

In describing his own passionate faith, Paul launches into a creed for the backward life:

> But whatever was to my profit I now consider loss for the sake of Christ. What is more, I consider everything a loss compared to the surpassing greatness of knowing Christ Jesus my Lord, for whose sake I have lost all things.
>
> Philippians 3:7–8

Translation: "All of my trophies, all of my accomplishments, all of my awards, all of my plaques, all of my money, all of my connections—I have considered all of it nothing, pointless, worthless, hollow, and empty compared to the mind-boggling phenomenon of knowing the God I'm made for." How backward! The things our world applauds, Paul rejects. Look at that verse again. Did Paul say, "I consider everything a loss compared to the surpassing greatness of *feeling* Christ Jesus my Lord?" No. His passion has nothing to do with his feelings and everything to do with knowing Jesus.

Paul doesn't go on to say, "I consider them rubbish, that I may *feel* Christ," but "that I may gain Christ" (v. 8). You can't miss Paul's language here: *rubbish* literally means "excrement, dung, manure" in the Greek language. It's not a nice word. It's an "in your face" word to shock us into reality. The backward life is not about sacrificing our lives for the hope of *feeling* him more but about refusing to be seduced by the ways of this world for the joy of having him, finding our satisfaction in him, holding him dearer.

Paul continues, "I consider them rubbish, that I may gain Christ and be found in him, not having a righteousness of my own that comes from the law, but that which is through faith in Christ—the righteousness that comes from God and is by faith" (Phil. 3:8–9). We can't get it right by following a bunch of do's and don'ts. Being made right with God comes from God, by faith in God.

Paul continues, "I want to know Christ and the power of his resurrection and the fellowship of sharing in his sufferings, becoming like him in his death, and so, somehow, to attain to the resurrection from the dead" (Phil. 3:10–11). Paul is saying, "I want to *know* Christ, not just feel him." Paul wants to know Jesus so intimately that he longs to experience Jesus' sufferings. Now that's backward. That's what the world would call "foolish."

Paul knows the conquering power of the resurrection. By passionate faith he welcomes the suffering, the chiseling into holiness, as one who is free from this world, preparing for the next.

Faith vs. Feeling

Okay, I've hammered hard on the "feelings" thing. But as I mentioned earlier, feelings, sweet emotions, are not bad! They're natural. We are emotional creatures. Sweet emotions for God are gifts when they move you to tears as you listen to the sermon, read a devotional book, or sing along with a worship song on your iPod. Sweet emotions for God are blessings when you feel the strong arms of Jesus around you and his breath upon you as you go about your day.

However, sweet emotions become bad when you depend on them to fuel your faith, your joy, your obedience, or your passion for Jesus. This is how I once lived my Christian life. As the feelings soared, so would my faith. My passion and commitment strengthened. Then as the feelings faded, so would everything else.

The lightbulb came on in my spiritual life when that truth claimed my heart. See, God allows the feelings for him to fade so that our walk with him is based only on what pleases and blesses his heart—our faith. Welcome and embrace those times of soaring feelings with joy and thanksgiving. But pursue God by faith. Plead with him to stir your heart more for him. Until then, earnestly seek him by faith.

My wife, Christie, is gorgeous and godly (I wanted to say she is "hot and holy," but she hates it when I say that). A month before our wedding we wrote our own vows to each other. I'm thankful to say that, like going to a fight where a hockey game breaks out, our marriage was a worship service where a wedding broke out. My vows to Christie were very practical. One of them stated, "This day and forever, Christie, I covenant to snuggle with you on the couch and not get preoccupied with ESPN or *The O'Reilly Factor*."

Have I always lived up to that vow? Um, no. I'm getting better, though. But do I always want to snuggle with my wife on the couch and "act all married"? No. Do I always want to watch ESPN and *The O'Reilly Factor*? Yes! Let me take it up a notch: do I always *feel* in love with my wife? No; nor does my wife always *feel* in love with me. But even when I don't feel like it, and even when I don't feel in love with Christie, I do things for her and with her—like washing dishes (I put them in the dishwasher) or snuggling on the couch (sometimes both on the same day)—until my sweet feelings for her are stirred again. Most times it's the commitment, the vow, that fuels the love. It's a marriage set in the concrete of a love commitment, not a marriage set in the sand of feelings of love.

It's no different with God's love for us. Do you think God always *feels* in love with us when we act the way we do, say the things we say, or think those unholy thoughts? I love my son intensely. But when he puts the remote control in the dog's water bowl for the thirteenth time, I don't *feel* so in love with him. But it doesn't change the *fact* that I love him deeply. God doesn't just love us through feelings—he loves us through Jesus. His love for us is fact and feeling. He loves us through his commitment to us and, yes, his feelings for us.

That's how it is with our love for God. When we don't feel in love with God, we seek him because he first sought us. We run to him because he first ran to us. We love him because he first loved us. We serve him, obey him, rejoice in him because his commitment to us in Christ and our commitment to him because of Christ fuels the relationship. That's faith. We seek God by faith, not according to how much we feel him but because faith pleases God. We seek God with all our hearts until our sweet emotions for him are stirred again.

Paul, with or without sweet emotions, presses on for the One he's made for and the life he's meant for: "Not that I have already obtained all this, or have already been made perfect, but I press on to take hold of that for which Christ Jesus took hold of me" (Phil. 3:12). It's easy to just read this and think, "Hooray for Paul; he's pressing on for Jesus . . . whatever that means." What does Paul mean by "press on"? He explains, "I have worked much harder, been in prison more frequently, been flogged [beaten with a whip full of glass, bone, and rock] more severely, and been exposed to death again and again. Five times I received from the Jews the forty lashes minus one" (2 Cor. 11:23–24). Prison? Beaten? Death? Paul isn't exactly talking about a Christian beach retreat here. He's talking about his backward life.

Paul also mentions, almost as an aside, that he received thirty-nine lashes from the brutal whip. Only thirty-nine lashes were given because it was believed that the fortieth lash would kill the victim. The Jews didn't want to kill Paul; they wanted to torture him for preaching Jesus as Messiah and Lord. They brutally beat him this way *five* different times. They would drag Paul out of his prison cell, beat him to a pulp with the thirty-nine lashes, and throw him back in prison. A while later, they would drag him back out of prison, whip him again with thirty-nine lashes, and throw him back in prison. Soon they would drag him out and beat him again . . . and they would beat him again . . . and they would whip him again, within a lash of his life. But still he says, "I press on."

Paul continues:

> Three times I was beaten with rods, once I was stoned, three times I was shipwrecked, I spent a night and a day in the open sea, I have been constantly on the move. I have been in danger from rivers, in danger from bandits, in danger from my own countrymen, in danger from Gentiles; in danger in the city, in danger in the country, in danger at sea; and in danger from false brothers. I have labored and toiled and have often gone without sleep; I have known hunger and thirst and have often gone without food; I have been cold and naked. Besides everything else, I face daily the pressure of my concern for all the churches. Who is weak, and I do not feel weak? Who is led into sin, and I do not inwardly burn?
>
> 2 Corinthians 11:25–29

I have to ask: Do you think Paul was feeling on fire for God during those experiences? Do you think Paul *felt* like pressing on?

But Paul lived by faith, not feeling.

Honestly, out of all Paul's experiences, the only thing I might be able to relate to in my life is the lack of sleep, or being hungry or cold, or feeling pressure. I get hungry when I don't get enough pizza, or I get tired when I stay up too late watching *Forensic Files*. I get cold because I turned my air conditioner up too high before I went to bed after staying up too late watching *Forensic Files*. I feel the pressure of meeting a deadline because I've procrastinated by watching reruns of *Forensic Files*. And let me tell you, then I don't feel on fire for God because of my own puny, self-imposed troubles. So can you imagine Paul?

I guarantee you Paul didn't wake up in his prison cell, with the flesh of his back shredded like paper, feeling so saved. I woke up a few mornings ago, as I do many mornings, not feeling so saved either. It all began when I clicked on an email attachment. Instantly a computer worm crawled its way into my laptop, locking up my whole system. I was up until the wee hours of the morning trying to figure out what to do, trying to get hold of a computer techie from Norton Antivirus. No luck.

I gave up and went to bed, but all night I felt like I was wrestling this gigantic worm in my sleep. I tossed and turned, kicked, sighed, and jerked the covers, while Christie was in peaceful slumber. On top of that, there was this hideous noise coming from our bedroom ceiling fan that sounded like someone strangling a cat.

I finally got up without turning on the light so I wouldn't wake Christie. I tried to eyeball what was wrong with the fan. Unable to see in the dark, of course, and very ticked off, I began grabbing at everything around the glass covering the lightbulb. I was turning screws, jerking the fan cord, and jiggling the light covering.

Then all of a sudden I got my hand a little too high, and "whap!" the fan raked my knuckles. After doing a tiptoe prancing ballet around the room in my boxers, biting my lip, I noticed that the fan had stopped shrieking. Satisfied, I lay back down with throbbing knuckles, hoping to get a couple hours of sleep, until . . . "rouw, raaeeek, rouw, raaaeeek"—the strangled cat was back.

I buried my head under my pillow, just wanting to scream.

For the rest of the night I wrestled with a gigantic worm, fought off a screaming cat, and ran for my life from a giant fan.

The next morning I didn't feel so on fire for God. I didn't feel so saved either. I didn't feel like reading my Bible. I didn't feel like praying. I didn't feel in love with my wife. But I went into my study (which is really our spare bedroom/storage room), sat down with the Bible in front of me, and whispered to God a weak prayer: "Lord, I'm tired. I'm frustrated. I'm bitter. I want to pout with you, Christie, and the whole world. I don't feel like reading your Word. I don't feel like really talking to you. Lord, I really just feel numb. But by *faith* I come to you, and I come bringing nothing but my need of you. Lord, by your grace, I *press on*."

The backward passion found in passionate faith can be summed up in three words: "I press on." Paul said it best,

> *I press on* to take hold of that for which Christ Jesus took hold of me. Brothers, I do not consider myself yet to have taken hold of it. But one thing I do: Forgetting what is behind and *straining* toward what is ahead, *I press on* toward the goal to win the prize for which God has called me heavenward in Christ Jesus.
>
> Philippians 3:12–14, emphasis added

You will most likely never face the forty lashes minus one, death by stoning, or beatings with rods. But it's possible someone could take the credit for your work, or your car's fuel pump could go out, costing you five hundred dollars that you don't have. You could get cut from the team or be stood up for a date. You could lose your job, your husband might miss your anniversary for the third year in a row, or you might never meet "the one." You might have a noisy ceiling fan that you want to rip out of the ceiling at 4:30 in the morning. If so, will you press on for Jesus? Or will you fumble the proverbial ball like our teenage friend who wrote me the email because all along you've lived for God by feelings instead of by faith?

To live the backward life you're meant for, you must have a backward passion for the God you're made for—a passion fueled by faith, not by feelings. It's a Lance Armstrong and a Ben Comen passion, an apostle Paul passion that presses on and strains toward the goal—not just any goal but the goal of knowing and having Jesus through faith. It's a passionate faith that says of Jesus, "I've got to have him!" no matter how you feel, no matter how much it hurts, and no matter how much it costs. It's a passionate faith that presses on.

THE BACKWARD HOPE

15

Happy Endings

> "Safe?...Who said anything about safe? 'Course he isn't safe.
> But he's good."
>
> Mr. Beaver describing the Christ-figure Aslan the lion
> in C. S. Lewis's *The Lion, the Witch and the Wardrobe*

My two favorite heroes growing up were Spiderman and Superman. I still have a pair of "Underoos" from my childhood to prove it. For those of you who don't have a clue about Underoos, they were basically underwear and T-shirts made to look like superhero uniforms. I had the Spiderman Underoos, which were blue underwear with red trim and a red T-shirt with the webbing printed on the front. But I could never decide whether my favorite superhero was Spiderman or Superman, so my mom got me a Superman cape to go along with my Spiderman Underoos.

Just about any summer afternoon you could drive past our home and see this pale white, dirty-kneed, bushy blond-headed kid running around the yard, darting between trees in his underwear with a red cape flapping behind him. Dogs, cats, and squirrels would run for their lives while the superhero, yours truly, punished the evil forces of his wicked sister. Just in case you're wondering, I stopped doing that last year.

What I loved most about the superhero stories was that no matter how terrible things got, the good guys always won. Spiderman and Superman always got the girl, and everything was made right in the end. There was always a happy ending.

Since the turn of the new century, we've heard a lot about heroes—the firemen and policemen of the September 11 terrorist attack on the World Trade Center, the astronauts of the Space Shuttle Columbia that disintegrated over Texas, and our American soldiers fighting for peace in Iraq.

Unlike fictional heroes, heroes in the real world die. With the realization that each of us will face crippling tragedies in our own lives, the most important question of our real life story becomes, "How will everything turn out in the end? Is there a happy ending?"

The Bible talks about heroes of faith who were real, ordinary human beings. What made them heroes was a hope and faith that was backward to this world. Meet Job. Job was one of those heroes whose hope didn't lie in the here and now. His hope was not based on positive thinking or some fantasy. His hope went beyond this world, resting in the one true Creator God of heaven and earth. The book of Job is a true story. It's a lesson about faith and its trials. It's real faith that allows us to embrace life fully—the good, the bad, and the ugly. It's a story about more than the faith of a man; it's about the sovereignty of his God. Job's faith is our faith, his hope our hope—that no matter what happens in our world or in our lives, for those who trust Jesus, God will make all things right in the end. It's the backward truth that on the other side of this world's sadness, trouble, and despair is the promise of a happy ending.

Backward Hope: God Is Sovereign in the Good

> In the land of Uz there lived a man whose name was Job. This man was blameless and upright; he feared God and shunned evil. He had seven sons and three daughters, and he owned seven thousand sheep, three thousand camels, five hundred yoke of oxen and five hundred donkeys, and had a large number of servants. He was the greatest man among all the people of the East.
>
> Job 1:1–5

Contrary to what many religious instructors teach, Job is not a book about why bad things happen to good people. Rather, it's a book that reveals what true faith looks like when bad things happen—a backward hope.

God spotlights Job's character—blameless, upright, feared God, shunned evil—then follows with details about the vast size of his family, wealth, and reputation. Does this mean then that great faith will bring health, wealth, and power? To hear many false teachers today, some of whom you may see on Christian television shows, you'd think the answer is yes. Not true. If that was what great faith in God was all about, who would long for heaven? Granted, there is a connection between obedience or devotion to God and his blessing. But God, out of his kindness and graciousness, also blesses rebellious and disobedient people: "He causes his sun to rise on the evil and the good, and sends rain on the righteous and unrighteous" (Matt. 5:45). Donald Trump is not a believer in Jesus Christ, yet he is one of the wealthiest men in the world. It has nothing to do with his "faith."

We can sometimes misunderstand a blessing and think that our action caused positive results. We got the job as a result of a good interview, or we got a promotion because of how many hours we put in at the office, or because we are so talented or gifted, or were in the right place at the right time, or were lucky. First of all, if God had a dictionary, you would never find the word *lucky*. Second, anything good we receive—financially, relationally, or materially—is not ultimately because of us or what we did, ever. It's because God chose to grant this to us by his designed means. If God ordains for a Southerner and a Yankee who live over a thousand miles away from each other to meet and marry, it will happen. If one's plan to go to New York and the other's plan for ministry abroad get in the way, he will rearrange those plans. No one and nothing can thwart God's plan. He is sovereign.

I consider myself blessed in so many ways. I'm sure Job considered himself blessed because of all the gifts God had given him. You have to wonder, though, if Job got caught up in his "blessings" and forgot God. Or could it be that Job was only devoted to God because of the gifts God had given him? Was Job's motive to love and obey God so that God would continue to bless him? What did Job love most, the gifts or the Giver?

According to the first chapter of Job, Satan presented himself to God, and God asked him, "Where have you come from?" (v. 7). Satan answered, "From roaming through the earth and going back and forth in it" (v. 7). Then God said, "Have you considered my servant Job? There is no one on earth like him; he is blameless and upright, a man who fears God and shuns evil" (v. 8). Leaning forward and narrowing his eyes, Satan challenges God, "Does Job fear God for nothing? . . . Have you not put a hedge around him and his household and everything he has? You have blessed the work of his hands, so that his flocks and herds are spread throughout the land. But stretch out your hand and strike everything he has, and he will surely curse you to your face" (Job 1:9–11).

Do you see what happened here? Satan's claim is just what we've been talking about—Satan tells God that Job is only devoted to God because of the gifts he has received. Satan accuses God of blessing Job to the point that Job can't help but love and adore God. "It's the gifts Job really loves, not you, God," Satan claims.

My dad trained himself to be a professional photographer. Within a few years, his photography business exploded, and he was booked years in advance to photograph weddings. He once told me that when he invested in his first camera, he prayed, "Lord, please just let me be good at this." And the Lord answered. But my dad will be the first to tell you that the gift God gave him soon became his god. As the business grew, he quit attending church, his health took a nosedive, and he suffered a heart attack at forty-nine years old. His health and twenty-something-year marriage to my mom lay in near ruins. He fell in love with the gift and forgot the Giver.

When I got serious about basketball in high school, I also prayed, "Lord, please let me be good at this." And God answered me too. Okay, I was never a superstar, not even close to being good enough to go to the NBA, but God allowed me a taste of popularity, accomplishment, and experiences that many people only dream about. But you guessed it: basketball became my god. I fell in love with the gift and forgot the Giver. I lived only for myself and my pleasures as a college basketball player. I basked in the little bit of glory that came my way. I basked in my glory and shunned God's glory. And if the game wasn't treating me well or I wasn't getting the attention I had once experienced, I would go into a funk and get mad at God!

Even now, the gift of ministry toes the line of becoming a god in my life. It's a battle. I come to God often and repent when I discover that I've loved my work more than I've loved him. Isn't it amazing that the work one does for God can actually become the "god" of one's life?

I have the same problem with my gifts of family, health, comfort, and security. I take these things for granted and nurture them with all my time and energy. I thank God for them but then get thrown into a quick "freak-out" phase when one of these areas is threatened. It is during the freak-out phase that I'm confronted with what I've loved more, treasured more, worshiped more—the gifts or God. How easy it is to fall in love with the gifts of God and forget the God of the gifts.

Backward Hope: God Is Sovereign in the Grief

Satan has declared to God that Job only seeks and loves God because of all that God has given Job. This is an accusation that God does not take lightly.

> The LORD said to Satan, "Very well, then, everything he has is in your hands, but on the man himself do not lay a finger." Then Satan went out from the presence of the LORD.
>
> Job 1:12

Let me prep you with this life-sustaining truth as we continue this story: God is sovereign in the grief. Satan is about to wreak havoc in Job's life. But also notice that nothing can take place against Job without first "passing across God's desk." God gave Satan permission with boundaries. Who has authority over Satan? God!

Christians will always debate whether or not disasters and terrorist attacks are satanic calamities. Whether they were caused by Satan, the curse of sin upon nature, or the sinfulness and fault of human beings (or all the above), we cannot know, for "the secret things belong to the LORD" (Deut. 29:29). But one thing I can tell you for sure: God doesn't say, "Oh my gosh! How did that happen? Someone get Gabriel on the phone!" God knew of the tragedies before the foundations of the world were laid, and in his mysterious will he allows them to happen. God can stop tragedies. And if Satan is the culprit, all God has to do is yank Satan's chain. Often God chooses not to for reasons we cannot understand.

God could have stopped the calamities against Job also. God "loosened Satan's chain," and what followed were three satanic and crippling right-left hooks that pinned Job against the ropes, and then the final knockout blow.

Right hook:

> One day when Job's sons and daughters were feasting and drinking wine at the oldest brother's house, a messenger came to Job and said,

"The oxen were plowing and the donkeys were grazing nearby, and the Sabeans attacked and carried them off. They put the servants to the sword, and I am the only one who has escaped to tell you!"

Job 1:13–15

Left hook:

While he was still speaking, another messenger came and said, "The fire of God fell from the sky and burned up the sheep and the servants, and I am the only one who has escaped to tell you!"

Job 1:16

Right hook:

While he was still speaking, another messenger came and said, "The Chaldeans formed three raiding parties and swept down on your camels and carried them off. They put the servants to the sword, and I am the only one who has escaped to tell you!"

Job 1:17

Job's property . . . destroyed. Job's servants . . . killed. Job's riches . . . gone. Then this—the knockout blow:

While he was still speaking, yet another messenger came and said, "Your sons and daughters were feasting and drinking wine at the oldest brother's house, when suddenly a mighty wind swept in from the desert and struck the four corners of the house. It collapsed on them and they are dead, and I am the only one who has escaped to tell you!"

Job 1:18–19

The ultimate tragedy occurs. A mammoth tornado drops from the sky, roaring in fury, snapping trees like celery, and crushes the house like tinfoil, and Job's sons and daughters along with it. I can remember my Grandmother Lockhart talking about a massive tornado hitting her little community of Shiloh, Alabama, when she was just a child. My great-great-great-grandmother, who was staying in the home of my great-great-aunt and uncle, lay sick in bed when the tornado hit. In the aftermath of the tornado, the home was destroyed.

When the storm subsided, other members of my family began searching for them, expecting the worst. Unbelievably, they found my great-great-great-grandmother in the middle of a nearby pasture, still lying on the mattress! She was unharmed. They also found my great-great-aunt and uncle there. Their barn had been completely destroyed, and they were found lying beneath some of the debris. They spent a few weeks in the hospital but fully recovered. The Bible that they kept in the drawer of their nightstand was also found in the middle of the rain-soaked, debris-ridden pasture. The Bible was found in perfect condition, dry as a bone!

I wonder if after Job received the horrific news, he might have fled with his servant to the rubble of the home. He probably searched for his kids, screaming out their names as the rain beat down on his wet back, pleading with God that they might still be alive. I can see him collapse in despair when he moves the debris to find all his children dead.

> At this, Job got up and tore his robe and shaved his head. Then he fell to the ground in worship and said: "Naked I came from my mother's womb, and naked I will depart. The LORD gave and the LORD has taken away; may the name of the LORD be praised." In all this, Job did not sin by charging God with wrongdoing.
>
> Job 1:20–21

Job must have wept in intense anguish, no doubt. But even in his bitter weeping and grief he worshiped. How? Why? He knew God was sovereign in his grief. He worshiped and said, "The LORD gave and the LORD has taken away" (v. 21). Knowing that God was sovereign, knowing that God was good, Job worshiped God by saying, "May the name of the LORD be praised" (v. 21). Job was saying,

"O God, I am crushed. But I know I have deserved nothing good from your hand, for I am a sinner. I know that I am nothing and have nothing without you. All that I had, even my children, were yours, O God. You chose to give them to me, and now you've chosen to take them from me. O my awesome, terrifying, and mysterious God, blessed be your name."

Is that backward or what? It's a holy fear and a backward hope in the sovereign God of heaven and earth, knowing that somehow God will make all things right and perfect in the end.

A Hero of Faith?

Job was a hero of faith, but he definitely wasn't perfect. He was human. No matter how godly his life or how backward his hope, he struggled deeply with the devastation that wrecked his life. After listening to friends give him poor advice about his life's situation, he turns his eyes to heaven and asks God the timeless and universal question of questions: "Why?" Job gathers his papers into his briefcase and goes off to heavenly court to present his case to God:

> If I have put my trust in gold or said to pure gold, "You are my security," if I have rejoiced over my great wealth, the fortune my hands had gained . . . then these also would be sins to be judged, for I would have been unfaithful to God on high. . . . I have not allowed my mouth to sin.
>
> Job 31:24–25, 28, 30

> Have I covered my transgressions like Adam, by hiding iniquity in my bosom?
>
> Job 31:33 NASB

> (Oh that I had someone to hear me! I sign now my defense—let the Almighty answer me.)
>
> Job 31:35

Basically, Job said, "God, if I loved and trusted the gifts (gold, wealth, fortune) more than you, if I had a mouth that cursed and rebelled against you, if I had secret sin I was trying to hide from you, then maybe, maybe I could understand my calamity. Do you hear me, God? Answer me, God, please! Why have you done this? Where are you? Why are you silent?"

Job daringly calls God to account. Finally, out of the silence, God takes center stage:

> Then the LORD answered Job out of the storm. He said: "Who is this that darkens my counsel with words without knowledge? Brace yourself like a man; I will question you, and you shall answer me. Where were you when I laid the earth's foundation? Tell me, if you understand. Who marked off its dimensions? Surely you know! Who stretched a measuring line across it? On what were its footings set, or who laid its cornerstone—while the morning stars sang together and all the angels shouted for joy? ... Do you know the laws of the heavens? Can you set up God's dominion over the earth? Can you raise your voice to the clouds and cover yourself with a flood of water? Do you send lightning bolts on their way? Do they report to you, 'Here we are'? Who endowed the heart with wisdom or gave understanding to the mind?"
>
> Job 38:1–7, 33–36

In other words, God says, "Job, who do you think you are? What do you know? To vent at me like you have, well, you must be God. You must have it all figured out. The world must center on you. Take a look around, Job—did you speak the earth into existence and hear the angels roar with joy when it happened? Had any lightning bolts shown up for work lately, Job?"

What could Job say to this staggeringly great God now? What would you expect Job to say? "But, but, but ... "? This is what he says:

Then Job answered the LORD: "I am unworthy—how can I reply to you? I put my hand over my mouth. I spoke once, but I have no answer—twice, but I will say no more."

Job 40:3–5

I know that you can do all things; no plan of yours can be thwarted. You asked, "Who is this that obscures my counsel without knowledge?" Surely I spoke of things I did not understand, things too wonderful for me to know. You said, "Listen now, and I will speak; I will question you, and you shall answer me." My ears had heard of you, but now my eyes have seen you. Therefore I despise myself and repent in dust and ashes.

Job 42:2–6

For three chapters God peppers Job with an avalanche of questions that leaves him stunned, shaking in his sandals. Job's focus turns from himself and his tragic life to God, who is infinitely greater than all of Job's circumstances. God opens Job's eyes to a new vision of who God is.

Did you notice God never answered Job's "why"? In the same way, we rarely get our "why" questions answered by God. Rather, God reminds us in no uncertain terms through Job that he is infinitely greater than our own thoughts and ways.

God does things and allows things that we, like Job, will never understand with our human limitations. Instead of explaining, God does something greater. He reveals the wonder of himself in his written Word. He displays himself—holy, awesome, terrifying, powerful, immense, and good.

C. S. Lewis's work *The Lion, the Witch and the Wardrobe* includes a scene in which two talking beavers are describing to the children the mighty lion Aslan—the Christ-figure in the book. The beavers' awesome description of the great lion makes the children hesitant to meet him and prompts one of the children to probe further about him. Susan asks the beavers,

"Is he—quite safe? I shall feel rather nervous about meeting a lion."

"That you will, dearie, and no mistake," said Mrs. Beaver, "if there's anyone who can appear before Aslan without their knees knocking, they're either braver than most or else just silly."

"Then he isn't safe?" said Lucy.

"Safe?" said Mr. Beaver. "Don't you hear what Mrs. Beaver tells you? Who said anything about safe? 'Course he isn't safe. But he's good. He's the King, I tell you."[1]

Nowhere in Scripture does God reveal himself as predictable or safe. God in his unfathomable wisdom moves in ways that to us seem to make no sense. But God is God, and we are not. Although God is not safe, like Aslan, he is good. Scripture makes this clear.

I am the LORD, and there is no other; apart from me there is no God. . . . I form the light and create darkness, I bring prosperity and create disaster; I, the LORD, do all these things.

Isaiah 45:5, 7

You are good, and what you do is good; teach me your decrees.

Psalm 119:68

Do not fear, for I am with you; do not be dismayed, for I am your God. I will strengthen you and help you; I will uphold you with my righteous right hand.

Isaiah 41:10

When you pass through the waters, I will be with you; and when you pass through the rivers, they will not sweep over you. When you walk through the fire, you will not be burned; the flames will not set you ablaze. For I am the LORD, your God, the Holy One of Israel, your Savior.

Isaiah 43:2–3

Do you trust God primarily because of your semi-painless life experience, or do you trust God because of who he is, regardless of your life experience? If your trust is only based on the good things you receive from him, what will happen to your faith when darkness falls? Will the tragedies that strike your life mean that God is not perfect, just, good, and loving?

Absolutely not.

But when you place your faith in God's goodness (all the good things you receive) rather than God's sovereignty, you end up with a yo-yo faith—a faith that's here one minute, gone the next. This yo-yo faith constantly questions life, both the here and now and the life to come. Backward hope in God is not grounded in experience but grounded in the character of God as revealed in Scripture. Backward hope is trusting God's heart when we are tempted to doubt his hand. In this backward hope of trusting God's heart, a joyful ending is guaranteed no matter how dark our earthly lives get. God is sovereign in the grief.

Backward Hope: God's Sovereignty in the End

Although God didn't answer Job's questions, he did something greater: he revealed his glory and wonder to Job and mercifully restored Job's faith and family again.

> The LORD made him prosperous again and gave him twice as much as he had before.... The LORD blessed the latter part of Job's life more than the first.... And so he died, old and full of years.
>
> Job 42:10, 12, 17

I have to admit that throughout most of my Christian life I've wondered what in the world these last few verses of Job really meant. The natural question that surfaces for me, and perhaps for you, is this: does faith in God that sustains us through tragedy eventually bring greater health and wealth? No. What it does mean is that no matter what happens in our lives, for those who trust in God, he will make everything right in the end. How can we know this for sure? We look to the cross of Jesus. Job didn't have what we do—the treasure of knowing that God too knows suffering through the sacrifice of his Son Jesus. For you and me, the cross is the light at the end of the tunnel of our darkness. Whatever questions may come from our pain and suffering, we have the cross of Jesus as our ultimate answer.

> For God so loved the world that he gave his one and only Son, that whoever believes in him shall not perish but have eternal life.
>
> John 3:16

> For this reason he [Jesus] had to be made like his brothers in every way, in order that he might become a merciful and faithful high priest in service to God, and that he might make atonement for the sins of the people. Because he himself suffered.
>
> Hebrews 2:17–18

> And we know that in all things God works for the good of those who love him, who have been called according to his purpose.
>
> Romans 8:28

The cross of Jesus reminds us that for those who believe in him, God will make all things right in the end.

> Now the dwelling of God is with men, and he will live with them. They will be his people, and God himself will be with them and be their God. He will wipe away every tear from their eyes. There will be no more death or mourning or crying or pain, for the old order of things has passed away.
>
> Revelation 21:3–4

During the summer of 2002, on a mission project in Matamoros, Mexico, I met a young couple, Jack and Jodie Simmons. We became instant friends and witnessed God do amazing things around us the entire week. Jodie was also in the beginning stages of her pregnancy, and she and Jack were giddy over the anticipated birth of their child.

Although we've recently reunited, after the project, I lost contact with Jack and Jodie, but they were never far from my thoughts. As I began a new year in graduate school, I met another couple on campus who were from the same church as Jack and Jodie. I asked how Jack and Jodie were doing and received some heartbreaking news in response. The baby girl that Jodie was carrying had been diagnosed with Trisomy 18. This condition is pretty much a death sentence. In most cases of Trisomy 18, the child is born severely deformed and only lives for a couple of minutes. So for around nine months Jodie carried this baby knowing that when she gave birth, the baby would die within minutes.

In their grief, Jack sat down in front of his computer and typed an email filled with terrible sorrow and pain yet threaded with amazing joy and trust in God. His email is the very portrait of backward hope in God.

Tuesday, September 10, 2002, 4:27 p.m.

Over the past month [Jodie] and I have been overwhelmed with the goodness and faithfulness of God working through His people. Upon hearing that our little girl was diagnosed with Trisomy 18, we cried out to God with anger, brokenness, and bitter sorrow. We felt like we had been the subjects of enough of God's lessons that can only come from suffering. It is as if we cried out to God, saying, "Look at our scars from the suffering that has already come from your hand. Haven't we learned enough through the losses and heartaches we have already been through?" But even as we pled our case before the King of Kings, we came to a greater understanding of the scars He bears for our sake. My wife lives with the fact that the birth of her child, that miraculous process which is meant to bring life and joy, will most likely bring suffering and death. Never would we even imagine this dark paradox. But the God who alone is wise has ordained this same dark paradox for the firstborn among all men, His only Son. Now, as we go to the doctor and see the growth and development of our child in the womb, all of our would-be joy is overshadowed with the dark certainty of death. In a similar way God the Father watched His Son mature, knowing that the more He grew in favor with God and man, the nearer the awful day of His crucifixion.

My personal prayer throughout college and even now has often been that of the apostle Paul in Philippians 3:10, "that I may know Him and the power of His resurrection and the fellowship of His sufferings." As God's Spirit reminds me of that prayer, I realize that there is no other way to really know the fellowship of His suffering but to suffer. Even as painful as this time is to us and our family, I know that this is only a bitter drop compared to the cup of suffering that God poured out on His Son. God had in sight the redemption of all His prized and beloved creation as He ordained the painful suffering of His only Son. What might God have in mind for us through suffering? We don't know—we can't imagine and we don't try. His thoughts are incomprehensibly above ours. We can only seek to emulate the servants of old as they dealt with suffering from the hand of the almighty.

Job, in all his trials and affliction, said, "The Lord giveth. The Lord taketh away. Blessed be the name of the Lord." Jesus Himself had the same outlook on suffering. In John 9, Jesus answered that the blind man suffered this affliction so that "the works of God might be displayed in him." Our desire is to have the same heart of understanding. Our certainty is that God will some way, somehow receive glory in our suffering. And our comfort is that He is the loving Redeemer. He is not absent in our suffering or unaffected by it, but He will redeem it—if not on this side of eternity, then [on] the other.

Through this God has not only broken us, but He has reshaped us as well. Before, it was nothing for me to pray to God, my Father. I have been doing this since I was a child. But in our suffering, I have come to the trembling understanding that my Father is the King. I knew that God was referred to as the King of Kings, but I never really understood or experienced this kind of relationship before. Upon hearing the doctor's preliminary diagnosis (before the results were certain), Jodie and I prayed with great brokenness and earnestness

like we have never prayed before. We prayed more passionately, with
more desire than we had prayed for anything before, that the doctor's
preliminary diagnosis would be proved wrong by more certain tests.
But God denied our request—our most heartfelt request—He denied
it. If God's greatest desire was for the happiness of His children, He
would have granted this request. I just didn't understand how God
could fail me now.

There is only one solution: God's greatest desire is not for the
happiness of His children. God's greatest desire is for His glory, for
Scripture even says that ALL things are from Him, through Him,
and to Him. God's universe does not revolve around my happiness
and desires. This universe and all that has been created revolves
around the majestic throne of the Almighty King. God is not the
celestial servant who exists to grant my wishes—He is the King of
Kings. He is the Great I Am.

For weeks I could not call God "Father" in prayer. In a sense my
soul trembled and I could only carefully and seriously address Him
as King. I was not comfortable in speaking with Him, for I was made
aware of His truly sovereign power, glory, and autonomy in light
of my fickle creatureliness. In a sense I was like a child of a most
decorated general who for the first time saw the breathtaking power
of his father's command in a war, and for a short time thereafter is
afraid to even speak to one with such sovereign authority. Even in
saying that, my joy in knowing Him is all the more rich, as I begin
to grasp the fact that my Father is the King.

We are able to wholeheartedly sing with immovable joy and hope
the words of this great hymn:

> And, Lord, haste the day
> When my faith shall be sight,
> The clouds be rolled back as a scroll
> The trump shall resound
> And the Lord shall descend,
> Even so, it is well with my soul.[2]

That's backward hope. The truth is that we don't live in a world
of make-believe where superheroes come and save the day. We live

in a world that is real—brutally real. But know this now and forevermore: We have a God who saves the day. He's the King, I tell you! And he's good.

How will the story of our lives play out? For those who trust in Jesus, God will make all things right in the end. And, as Jack said, "our comfort is that He is the loving Redeemer. He is not absent in our suffering or unaffected by it, but He will redeem it—if not on this side of eternity, then [on] the other."

Conclusion

Back in January 2004, I was at work in my other office—the coffee shop at Books-A-Million—writing material for *The Backward Life*. I overheard a young man loudly complimenting the barista behind the coffee counter on how nice she was to him and others. I looked up to notice that the young man, maybe in his early twenties, had Down syndrome.

He eventually made his way to a table, reached into his backpack, pulled out a Bible, and opened it with the same excitement that I have when I open a box of Froot Loops. Alongside his Bible he took out a pencil and opened a little notebook of questions. He then got up and went back to the barista and asked her if she could help him find the book of First Corinthians. I chuckled at how the lady stared at him with question marks in her pupils, but also at how confident and excited he was in asking the lady to help him. She was nice but didn't know quite what to do with him. So she just nodded and kind of turned her back. He returned to his seat for a moment, only then to snag another girl walking by and ask for her help in finding another book of the Bible. (He liked the ladies, you can't blame him.) A few minutes after this encounter, he was up again, back up to the barista, asking for her help with a specific question about the Bible (which she couldn't answer).

Although he really wasn't getting the help he sought (something tells me he really didn't need the help), he was making the whole coffee shop and the bestseller section aware of Jesus. After the barista tried helping him with his question, he said, "You are such a very sweet lady. I bet you love Jesus, don't you."

"Excuse me?" she asked.

"I bet you love Jesus, don't you. You're so nice."

I was sitting over in the corner, taking in the scene. I didn't want him to notice me and my Bible. He was *loud*. And I knew he would erupt if he saw me with my Bible. So I kept my hat pulled down low on my forehead, trying to hide my eyes.

As he turned back toward his seat, we made eye contact. He smiled from ear to ear. My first thought was, *Uh-oh*.

"Hello, my name is Ben, how are you?" he bellowed across two tables.

"I'm great, my friend, how are you?" I answered.

He walked over to me and asked, "Whatcha working on?"

"Oh, I'm just writing some stuff on what it means to follow Jesus."

"Really?!" he shouted. "Will you read it to me? Can I sit down?"

"Sure," I said.

Let me remind you, Ben had a set of lungs on him. He spoke a few decibels higher than anyone in the whole place. But everything he said was so joyful, positive, encouraging, sincere, and Jesus-filled. Down he sat, and I read a chapter to him out of *The Backward Life* draft. Every time I read a Scripture within the chapter, he would "mmm" and "aaah." He stopped me once to say, "Jarrod, this is really speaking to my heart. I have struggled with that in my life, and you have really helped me." I smiled, amazed at his sincerity and understanding, while also thankful for his merciful and encouraging comments, then I read on. When I finished, he said, "Thank you for letting me sit with you and for reading to me. Can I pray for you?" "Please do," I answered, with my face turning a little red. I was caught a bit off guard. He turned the volume up even louder when he launched into pleas to God for me. I wanted to crawl under the table. I started sweating. Everyone was staring. By the time Ben was done, though, he had prayed over my life, my family, my ministry, the book, my future, and our new friendship. And any self-consciousness about my appearance, and what people in the coffee shop thought about him and me, melted away. It was unbelievable. We had church right there in the Books-A-Million coffee shop.

After praying he got up to leave, and as he walked out of the coffee shop he shouted, "Jarrod, I have a verse for you—Romans 5:8." I smiled and said in a forced tone, "Thank you, brother!" I sat there for a moment, trying to take in all that had just happened. I got out my Bible and turned to Romans 5:8: "But God demonstrates His own love toward us, in that while we were sinners, Christ died for us" (NASB).

I looked back toward the doors, and Ben was walking toward me again. We smiled at each other again, and I whispered, "Uh-oh."

He said, "Jarrod, I just wanted to thank you again for letting me pray for you. You are so nice, you're a handsome man, I like your fleece sweatshirt."

My face was glowing red now like a taillight. So bright was my face, flies were starting to swarm around my head. As all eyes looked toward us (as they had been doing for the last fifteen minutes), I very embarrassingly laughed and responded with the first thing that came to my mind. "Wow, brother, um, ahem, uh, thank you so much. I, um, I like your sweater."

Then, as he again turned to leave, he unashamedly said to me, "I love you, Jarrod, I'll be praying for you."

"I love you too, brother," I proudly replied.

When Benjamin got to the door he turned around *again* and shouted, "Jarrod . . . 'Be still and know that I am God.'" And with that final word from Psalm 46:10, he was gone.

And I couldn't wait to get home and tell Christie that I had just met Jesus in Books-A-Million.

Leading up to the new year, I had been thinking and praying about what more God wanted of me, and how much more like Christ—backward—God wanted to make me. With that in mind, I left about thirty minutes later, still thinking about my encounter with Benjamin. Driving home, I realized that God had sent me a living, breathing example to my prayer—Ben. In other words, like Ben, I want to be overflowing with a contagious and uninhibited joy in God. With a childlike faith I want to open God's Word and read it with giddiness. With reckless abandon, I want to passionately live for Jesus and share Jesus with anybody and everybody, anywhere and everywhere. I want to be an unrestrained encourager of people to seek Jesus with all their might. I want to love people even when it hurts, even when they turn their back on me. I want to sincerely pour out my heart for people in prayer, whether in private or with them in the middle of a coffee shop. I want to be more positive about everything in general. I want to live a life radically backward to this world and more different than anyone has ever seen, for Jesus' sake, for people's souls, and for God's glory. I want to be backward! I want to be just like Ben. No, I want to be just like Jesus.

What about you?

Notes

Epigraph

Merriam-Webster's Collegiate Dictionary, 11th ed., s.v. "Backward."

Chapter 2: Me, Me, Me

1. Wayne Martindale and Jerry Root, eds., *The Quotable Lewis* (Wheaton: Tyndale, 1990), 352.

2. This story is told in my own words as heard from Dave Stone, Southeast Christian Church, Louisville, KY, 2000. Sermon series: "Luke: Jesus Ruler of My Personality"; sermon title: "Sincerity"; September 17, 2000.

3. Ravi Zacharias, "The Lostness of Man." Sermon done at Billy Graham conference.

Chapter 3: I'm Made for *This*?

1. Jim Meehan, *Spokesman-Review*, August 1, 2003, C1.

Chapter 4: Will the Real God Please Stand Up?

1. Olivia Barker, "Madonna Has Faith on a String: Celebs Find Spirituality in Mystical Kabbalah," *USA Today*, May 26, 2004.

2. Angi Ma Wang, *Feng Shui: Do's and Taboos* (North Adams, MA: Storey Books, 2000), 45.

3. Ibid., copyright page.

Chapter 6: Gloriously Ruined

1. John Piper, "Holy, Holy, Holy Is the Lord of Hosts," audiotape of sermon preached at Bethlehem Baptist Church, Minneapolis, January 1, 1984.

2. Ibid.

3. Joni Eareckson Tada and Steven Estes, *When God Weeps: Why Our Sufferings Matter to the Almighty* (Grand Rapids: Zondervan, 1997), 53–54.

Chapter 8: Just Because

1. Andrew Guy Jr., "Are They for Real?: Famous Couples Practice Love Hollywood-Style," *Houston Chronicle*, September 16, 2003.
2. Piper, "Holy, Holy, Holy Is the Lord of Hosts."
3. Ravi Zacharias, Ravi Zacharias International Ministries, November 4, 2004, www.rzim.org/radio/archives.pnp?p=LMPTQV=detail&id=3.
4. Richard Stengel, "Miracle Girl," *Time*, August 31, 1987, 15.

Chapter 9: That's Incredible

1. For further study, see discussions in Craig's books: *Assessing the New Testament Evidence for the Historicity of the Resurrection of Jesus* (Lewiston, NY: The Edwin Mellen Press, 1989) and *Reasonable Faith: Christian Truth and Apologetics*, rev. ed. (Wheaton: Crossway, 1994).
2. William Lane Craig, "Rediscovering the Historical Jesus: The Evidence for Jesus," *Faith & Mission* 15, no. 2 (Spring 1998): 24.
3. John Ankerberg, "Did Jesus Rise from the Dead?" *The John Ankerberg Show*, videocassette 1 of 2. Produced and directed by John Ankerberg (Chattanooga, TN: Ankerberg Theological Institute, 2000).

Chapter 10: The Power of a Touch

1. Philip Yancey, *The Jesus I Never Knew* (Grand Rapids: Zondervan, 1995), 144.
2. George Bernard Shaw, *Man and Superman*, Act 4, stanza 369, www.bartleby.com.
3. Matt Damon, "There Is Another Way to Live: Interview with Matt Damon," interview by Dotson Rader, *Parade*, November 30, 2003, 6. Also available online at http://www.fortunecity.com/lavender/fullmonty/282/paradeinterview.html.

Chapter 11: Backward Loving

1. J. F. Walvoord, *The Bible Knowledge Commentary: An Exposition of the Scriptures*, CD-ROM (Wheaton: Victor Books, 1985).
2. John MacArthur, "Essentials for Growth in Godliness—Part 2," sermon at Grace Community Church, Sun Valley, California, 1988, text available online at http://www.biblebb.com/files/MAC/50-6.htm.
3. Bob Minzesheimer, "Back to the Beach: In 'Shark Trouble,' 'Jaws' Author Takes Their Side," *USA Today*, May 23, 2002.
4. Wayne Holmes, "Coming Alongside Our Kids," *Heartlight*, September 21, 2003, http://www.heartlight.org/articles/200309/20030921_alongside.html.

Chapter 12: The Backward Truth

1. If the monk had never heard of Jesus, his fate would be the same. That's not a popular truth. But moods may change, truth does not. Think about it. If the monk would still go to heaven without ever having heard of Jesus, we'd better quit commissioning missionaries to the unreached people groups. In other words, if a missionary shares the gospel and an unreached

people rejects the message, they will go to hell. So why preach the message with the risk that they'll reject it, eternally condemning their souls, if they'd go to heaven having never heard the message? If the monk ultimately sought truth, God would have sent him missionaries to preach the gospel, and upon his belief he'd be saved (see Romans 10:14–16).

2. D. A. Carson, *The Gagging of God: Christianity Confronts Pluralism* (Grand Rapids: Zondervan, 1996).

Chapter 13: The Backward Mind

1. The Associated Press, "Headless Chicken Saluted in Sculpture," *Birmingham News*, April 1, 2000. Also see http://www.miketheheadlesschicken.org.

Chapter 14: The Backward Faith

1. Rick Reilly, "Worth the Wait," *Sports Illustrated*, October 20, 2003, 76, available online at http://premium.si.cnn.com/pr/subs/siexclusive/rick_reilly/2003/10/13/reilly1020/index.html.

2. Ibid.

3. Ibid.

Chapter 15: Happy Endings

1. C. S. Lewis, *The Lion, the Witch and the Wardrobe* (New York: Harper Trophy, 1978), 86.

2. Jack and Jodie Simmons, September 10, 2002, personal email. Used by permission.

Meet Jarrod Jones

Jarrod Jones speaks more than one hundred times a year at churches, conferences, festivals, and ministry events. Represented by Vertical Ministries (www.verticalministries.com), his ministry extends throughout the United States and Canada.

In 2003 Jarrod graduated from Southern Baptist Theological Seminary at Louisville, Kentucky, with his masters of divinity degree. He also attended and played NCAA Division I basketball at Samford University, graduating in 1995 with a bachelor's degree in human development and family studies.

Jarrod and his wife, Christie, live with their sons, Josiah and Titus, and their Chihuahua, Tidbit, in Birmingham, Alabama. Jarrod's favorite family activities include eating extra-hot honey-barbeque buffalo wings and wrestling his sons on the living room floor.

Praise for Jarrod Jones

"Jarrod teaches the Bible to audiences with authority and passion. He speaks not only to their intellect but also to their emotions. Through his impassioned talks, I have seen many moved not only to tears but also to spiritual decisions."

Joe Botti, Xenos Christian Fellowship, Columbus, Ohio

"Jarrod did a wonderful job! He speaks the truth and stays true to the Word."

Louis Mizell, First Baptist Church, Lindale, TX

"Jarrod spends time with the teens, listening to them and engaging them in conversation, loving on them with the love of Christ. He truly is a man after God's own heart!"

Tracy Geglein, North United Methodist Church,
Madison, Indiana

To order a workbook for *The Backward Life* that's ideal for Bible study groups, or to find out more about the book, go to www.back wardlife.com.

For more on Jarrod's speaking schedule go to www.jarrodjones. com. If you're interested in scheduling Jarrod to speak to your group, please call 866-367-5333 or send an email to info@verticalministries. com and mention Jarrod Jones.

Revell

www.revellbooks.com